Modern Critical Views

Chinua Achebe
Henry Adams
Aeschylus
S. Y. Agnon
Edward Albee
Raphael Alberti
Louisa May Alcott
A. R. Ammons
Sherwood Anderson
Aristophanes
Matthew Arnold
Antonin Artaud
John Ashbery
Margaret Atwood
W. H. Auden
Jane Austen
Isaac Babel
Sir Francis Bacon
James Baldwin
Honoré de Balzac
John Barth
Donald Barthelme
Charles Baudelaire
Simone de Beauvoir
Samuel Beckett
Saul Bellow
Thomas Berger
John Berryman
The Bible
Elizabeth Bishop
William Blake
Giovanni Boccaccio
Heinrich Böll
Jorge Luis Borges
Elizabeth Bowen
Bertolt Brecht
The Brontës
Charles Brockden Brown
Sterling Brown
Robert Browning
Martin Buber
John Bunyan
Anthony Burgess
Kenneth Burke
Robert Burns
William Burroughs
George Gordon, Lord
    Byron
Pedro Calderón de la Barca
Italo Calvino
Albert Camus
Canadian Poetry: Modern
    and Contemporary
Canadian Poetry through
    E. J. Pratt
Thomas Carlyle
Alejo Carpentier
Lewis Carroll
Willa Cather
Louis-Ferdinand Céline
Miguel de Cervantes

Geoffrey Chaucer
John Cheever
Anton Chekhov
Kate Chopin
Chrétien de Troyes
Agatha Christie
Samuel Taylor Coleridge
Colette
William Congreve & the
    Restoration Dramatists
Joseph Conrad
Contemporary Poets
James Fenimore Cooper
Pierre Corneille
Julio Cortázar
Hart Crane
Stephen Crane
e. e. cummings
Dante
Robertson Davies
Daniel Defoe
Philip K. Dick
Charles Dickens
James Dickey
Emily Dickinson
Denis Diderot
Isak Dinesen
E. L. Doctorow
John Donne & the
    Seventeenth-Century
    Metaphysical Poets
John Dos Passos
Fyodor Dostoevsky
Frederick Douglass
Theodore Dreiser
John Dryden
W. E. B. Du Bois
Lawrence Durrell
George Eliot
T. S. Eliot
Elizabethan Dramatists
Ralph Ellison
Ralph Waldo Emerson
Euripides
William Faulkner
Henry Fielding
F. Scott Fitzgerald
Gustave Flaubert
E. M. Forster
John Fowles
Sigmund Freud
Robert Frost
Northrop Frye
Carlos Fuentes
William Gaddis
Federico García Lorca
Gabriel García Márquez
André Gide
W. S. Gilbert
Allen Ginsberg
J. W. von Goethe

Nikolai Gogol
William Golding
Oliver Goldsmith
Mary Gordon
Günther Grass
Robert Graves
Graham Greene
Thomas Hardy
Nathaniel Hawthorne
William Hazlitt
H. D.
Seamus Heaney
Lillian Hellman
Ernest Hemingway
Hermann Hesse
Geoffrey Hill
Friedrich Hölderlin
Homer
A. D. Hope
Gerard Manley Hopkins
Horace
A. E. Housman
William Dean Howells
Langston Hughes
Ted Hughes
Victor Hugo
Zora Neale Hurston
Aldous Huxley
Henrik Ibsen
Eugène Ionesco
Washington Irving
Henry James
Dr. Samuel Johnson and
    James Boswell
Ben Jonson
James Joyce
Carl Gustav Jung
Franz Kafka
Yasonari Kawabata
John Keats
Søren Kierkegaard
Rudyard Kipling
Melanie Klein
Heinrich von Kleist
Philip Larkin
D. H. Lawrence
John le Carré
Ursula K. Le Guin
Giacomo Leopardi
Doris Lessing
Sinclair Lewis
Jack London
Robert Lowell
Malcolm Lowry
Carson McCullers
Norman Mailer
Bernard Malamud
Stéphane Mallarmé
Sir Thomas Malory
André Malraux
Thomas Mann

Modern Critical Views

Modern Critical Views

LUIGI PIRANDELLO

Edited and with an introduction by
Harold Bloom
Sterling Professor of the Humanities
Yale University

CHELSEA HOUSE PUBLISHERS
New York ◊ Philadelphia

Printed and bound in the United States of America

10   9   8   7   6   5   4   3   2   1

∞The paper used in this publication meets the minimum
requirements of the American National Standard for
Permanence of Paper for Printed Library Materials,
Z39.48-1984.

Library of Congress Cataloging-in-Publication Data

Luigi Pirandello.
    (Modern critical views)
    Bibliography: p.
    Includes index.
    Summary: A collection of critical essays on the
Italian dramatist and his works arranged in chronological
order of publication.
    1. Pirandello, Luigi, 1867–1936—Criticism and
interpretation. [1. Pirandello, Luigi, 1867–1936—
Criticism and interpretation. 2. Italian literature—
History and criticism] I. Bloom, Harold. II. Series.
PQ4835.I7Z66487   1988   852'.912   87–27746
ISBN 1–55546–307–X

Contents

Editor's Note

This book brings together a representative selection of the best criticism available in English on the work of the modern Italian dramatist Luigi Pirandello. The critical essays are reprinted here in the chronological order of their original publication. I am grateful to Edward Jefferson for his judgment and erudition in assisting me to edit this volume.

My introduction speculates as to how Pirandello's plays revive the ancient Sicilian art of rhetoric, with its implicit identification of psychology and figurative language. Francis Fergusson's essay begins the chronological sequence by praising Pirandello as the forerunner of Yeats, Lorca, and Cocteau in starting again the search "for a modern poetry of the theater," with *Six Characters in Search of an Author* as an instance of a play whose action "takes the stage."

The dean of Pirandello critics, Eric Bentley, analyzes Pirandello's parody of *Hamlet, Henry IV*, as a tragic farce and as a version of Pirandello's obsessive pattern in which the wicked or trivial characters seek the truth while the serious figures seek love, only to find, for psychological reasons, that it has become impossible for them. Pirandello's nameless protagonist, at the close, "has reduced himself to an ultimate misery."

Pirandello's theory of "humorism" is masterfully expounded by Dante della Terza, who states the dramatist's conviction that the world exists yet is not meaningful and finds this the ultimate basis for Pirandello's art, "in which the spoken word becomes the character's last frontier of self-defense, his only possible action." Richard Gilman, in an overview of Pirandello's achievement, gives an appreciation of how Pirandello teaches us that "Illusion—artifice, formal pretense—is an aspect of reality, a means of expressing reality's insufficiency."

The use of paradox in Pirandello's drama is seen by Anne Paolucci as culminating in the nameless protagonist of *Henry IV*, "who comes closest to identification with Pirandello himself," presumably as Hamlet approached an identity with Shakespeare. The antimetaphysics of Pirandello's theatre are interpreted by Giovanni Sinicropi as centering upon an absolute refusal of the present and so of presence, in an anticipation of the rhetorical stance of Jacques Derrida.

Douglas Radcliff-Umstead, writing on Pirandello's novel *The Late Mattia Pascal,* finds in its intricate evasions of an inauthentic social reality a characteristic pattern that will receive dramatic embodiment in the author's later work in the theatre. The early Sicilian plays are studied by Olga Ragusa, who finds in them the crucial Sicilian characteristics of repression and the explosive violence that ensues from the return of the repressed.

In another overview, Maurice Valency traces the development of Pirandello's new conception of theatre from his acquaintance with such contemporary playwrights as Luigi Chiarelli and Rosso di San Secondo to the threshold of Artaud and Brecht in *Each in His Way.* Susan Bassnett-McGuire concludes this volume with a consideration of Pirandello's "Myth plays," *The New Colony* and *The Mountain Giants,* the first exposing the illusions of the social myth and the other revealing a triumph of the myth of art, but a triumph that is also a tragedy.

Introduction

Rhetoric, in its origins, was a Sicilian art, and it is fitting that the most rhetorical of modern dramatists, Luigi Pirandello, was also a Sicilian. The founder of rhetoric was the Sicilian shaman Empedocles, who preceded Plato in attempting to transform language from *doxa* (opinion) to truth, from the image-thinking of poetry to the concept-thinking of philosophy. Yet rhetoric stubbornly remained poetic, the instrument of a will-to-identity rather than a knower/known dualism. Gorgias, the Sicilian sophist who followed Empedocles, used rhetoric as Pirandello did, to enchant the audience into a realization of the antithetical nature of all truth. Plato, opposing this relativism, brought psychology and rhetoric overtly closer, but in essence they seem to me always one, with ancient and Renaissance cosmology making a third. In Pirandello, the Sicilian identity of rhetoric, psychology, and cosmology is confirmed. Though I agree with Eric Bentley, Pirandello's canonical critic, that the dramatist of *Henry IV* and *Six Characters in Search of an Author* is an Ibsenite, I find Pirandello closest to Gorgias. Pirandello is the playwright-as-sophist, leading us to the relativity of all truth, through an antithetical style.

An opportunistic perspectivism, *kairos*, is the occasion for the Pirandello drama as it was for the Gorgias oration. Bentley acutely notes the high rhetoricity of Pirandello, which masks as an antirhetoric but is a stormy counter-rhetoric.

> His strongest weapon is his prose. Its torrential eloquence and pungent force are unique in the whole range of modern drama, and recall the Elizabethans (in contrast with our verse playwrights who imitate the Elizabethans and do not in the least recall them). He gets effects that one would not have thought possible to colloquial prose, thus compelling us to reopen the discussion of

1

poetry and drama, in which it has always been assumed that prose was a limitation.

Bentley quotes Pirandello on his own achievement, in a passage that carries us back to ancient Sicily and Gorgias's insistence upon *kairos*, the opportune word for the opportune moment, here in Pirandello "the word that will be the action . . . the living word . . . the immediate expression." One wonders if there is an element in Sicilian culture, repressive and sublimely explosive, that guarantees this continuity with ancient rhetoric even as Pirandello expounds his idea of dramatic composition:

> So that the characters may leap from the written pages alive and self-propelled, the playwright needs to find the word that will be the action itself spoken, the living word that moves, the immediate expression, having the same nature as the act itself, the unique expression that cannot but be this—that is, appropriate to this given character in this given situation; words, expressions, which are not invented but are born, when the author has identified himself with his creature to the point of feeling it as it feels itself, wishing it as it wishes itself.

An art this rhetorical carries us back to Jacobean drama, the closest modern equivalent of which I would locate in Pirandello's extraordinary *Henry IV* (1922), though Beckett's *Endgame* comes to mind as an even darker rival. If Pirandello's *Henry IV,* generally regarded as a tragical farce, is also to be granted the status of tragedy, of a modern *Hamlet,* it can only be if the representation of the nameless nobleman, Pirandello's protagonist, possesses the aesthetic dignity appropriate to tragic art. That dignity turns upon his rhetorical persuasiveness, since the nameless one *wants* to be a tragic hero. Bentley, with great shrewdness, notes that Pirandello is not persuaded by his own creature:

> The protagonist insists on tragedy; the author does not. The protagonist is a character in search of the tragic poet: such is Pirandello's subject, which therefore comes out absurd, grotesque, tragicomic.

Dialectically, Bentley is accurate, and I think he interprets the play as Pirandello wished it to be interpreted. But strong rhetoric resists our will-to-power when we seek to interpret it, and the nameless one is a powerful rhetorician. Bentley thinks him essentially mad and regards his final stabbing of Belcredi as a crime. Belcredi is a skeptic and a jokester; in the world of *Henry IV* that marks him for death. Against such a view, Bentley argues that "this is not tragedy, a heroic genre, but post-Dostoevski psychological drama showing the decline and fall of a man through mental sickness to crime." Time sustains Bentley, but then tragedy is no longer a heroic genre for us. It still is for the nameless one who has played at being Henry IV, and I am on his side as against Bentley and Pirandello, whose cruel joke it is that this character has found the wrong author at the wrong time.

That still leaves us with the puzzle of aesthetic dignity in *Henry IV*. The nameless one surely is in search of Kleist to serve as his author, or if he cannot get Kleist, he would take Schiller. Pirandello, the Sicilian sophist, has created an Idealist protagonist for his Materialist play, and I suspect that the nameless one stabs Belcredi as a substitute for Pirandello himself, for having failed to let himself become a Kleist or a Schiller. If the nameless one is our Hamlet, then Pirandello is our Claudius in this clash of mighty opposites. *Henry IV* becomes its protagonist's revenge upon Pirandello for refusing to write a tragedy rather than a farce. And yet the grand rhetoric of this Sicilian descendant of Empedocles and Gorgias takes a subtler and more beautiful revenge. Few moments in modern drama have the poignance of the vision Pirandello grants us of the nameless one and his inadequate retainers sitting together in the lamplight, with the marvelous antithesis of the actors, acting the part of acting Henry IV and his retainers, set against the rhetoric, at once ironic and opportunistic, of the nameless Idealist:

> HENRY IV: Ah, a little light! Sit there around the table, no, not like that; in an elegant, easy, manner! . . . (*To Harold.*) Yes, you, like that! (*Poses him.*) (*Then to Berthold.*) You, so! . . . and I, here! (*Sits opposite them.*) We could do with a little decorative moonlight. It's very useful for us, the moonlight. I feel a real necessity for it, and pass a lot of time looking up at the moon from my window. Who would think, to look at her that she knows that eight hundred years have passed, and that I, seated at the window, cannot really be Henry IV gazing at the moon like any poor devil? But, look, look! See what a magnificent might scene we have here: the emperor surrounded by his faithful counsellors! . . . How do you like it?

How do we like it? Despite the overt irony, it seems too tragic for farce, but perhaps only for this single moment. Pirandello, in his counter-rhetoric, does remain an ancient Sicilian rhetorician and charms us into relativity by the incantation of his antitheses. His influence upon other dramatists came through his innovations as a counter-illusionist, but his continued influence upon us is rhetorical as well as dramatic.

FRANCIS FERGUSSON

Action as Theatrical: Six Characters in Search of an Author

There is a kinship between what I have called the Shavian theatricality, especially as it emerges in the later plays, and the much deeper, more consistent and more objective theatrical forms of Pirandello. Shaw as theater artist seems to have been feeling for something which Pirandello achieved: the restoration of the ancient magic of "two boards and a passion," frankly placed in the glare of the stage lights and the eye of the audience. In both theaters, the human is caught rationalizing there in the bright void. But Pirandello, having the seriousness of the artist, presents this farcical-terrible vision with finality and in an integral theatrical form; while in Shaw's complex case the artist is always being thwarted by the drawing-room entertainer or dismissed as romantic by the Fabian optimist or the morally fit man of good will. It is therefore Pirandello that one must study in order to see how the contemporary idea of a theater (as held by its most accomplished masters) emerged from nineteenth century Realism and Romanticism, including and transcending those genres as well as Shaw's solitary farce-of-rationalizing.

Six Characters is a convenient example of Pirandello's art: his most famous work, and his first unqualified success. I here remind the reader of the main outlines of its plot.

When the play begins, the curtain is up, the set is stacked against the stage-wall, and a troupe of actors with their director is rehearsing a new play by Pirandello. The rehearsal is interrupted by the arrival of a family in deep mourning: Father, Mother, grown Daughter and Son, and two younger children. These are the "characters"—fictions of the imagination of an author who has refused to write their story—and they have come to get their story or their drama somehow realized. They ask the actors to perform it instead of the play by Pirandello which they had started to rehearse. From this point,

---

From *The Idea of a Theater.* © 1949, 1977 by Princeton University Press.

the play develops on several levels of make-believe. There is the struggle of the "characters" against the actors and their director, who find the story confusing, or boring, or not good box-office. There is the more savage struggle between the various characters, who cannot agree about the shape, the meaning, or even the facts of their story, for each has rationalized, or mythicized it, in his own way. A few sordid facts emerge: the Father had sent the Mother away to live with another man, whom, he thought, she would love better, and the three younger children are hers by this other man. Hovering near the family, watching its life at a little distance, the Father had met his wife's Daughter at a house of assignation, Madame Pace's dress shop. Complicated jealousies had developed among the four children of the double brood, culminating in the suicide of the little boy. The crucial episodes are re-enacted by the tormented and disputing characters in order to show the actors what the story is. When the suicide of the little boy comes up again, by a sort of hellish eternal recurrence, all breaks up in confusion—the fictive characters more real, in their conscious suffering, than the flesh-and-blood acting company.

The story of the six characters, as we gradually make it out, is melodramatic and sensational. The disputes which break out from time to time about "idea and reality," "life and art," and the like, are based on paradoxes in the Shavian manner: romantically unresolved ambiguities. The whole work may seem, at first sight, to be shop-worn in its ideas and, in its dramaturgy, hardly more than a complex piece of theatrical trickery. When it first appeared, in 1921, some critics were disposed to dismiss it in this way. But the fine productions which it received all over the world gradually revealed its true power and interest, which is not in the literal story of the characters, nor in the bright, paradoxical play of ideas, but in the original sense of action underlying the whole play. Pirandello has explained all this with great clarity in the preface he wrote in 1930 for the ninth edition. This preface is almost as important as the play. It deserves to rank with Cocteau's *Call to Order* and Eliot's *Dialogue on Dramatic Poetry,* as one of the works which endeavor to lay the basis for a contemporary theory of drama.

The action of the play is "to take the stage"—with all that this suggestive phrase implies. The real actors and the director want to take it for the realistic purposes—vain or (with the box-office in mind) venal—of their rehearsal. Each of the characters wants to take it for the rationalized myth which is, or would be, his very being. Pirandello sees human life itself as theatrical: as aiming at, and only to be realized in, the tragic epiphany. He inverts the convention of modern realism; instead of pretending that the stage is not the stage at all, but the familiar parlor, he pretends that the familiar parlor is not real, but a stage, containing many "realities." This is, of course, a narrow and violently idealist view of human life and action; but if held with Pirandello's strict consistency, it cuts deep—very much as the narrow idea of the Baroque theater, to which it is so closely akin, cuts deep, enabling a Racine to search and reveal the heart. Certainly it is a version of action which enables Pirandello to bring the stage itself alive at levels of awareness far beyond those of modern realism.

By the time Pirandello wrote the preface to his play, he had had time to read criticisms of it from all over the world, and to discover how its audiences had interpreted it. These audiences were trained in the modes of understanding of modern realism, and they almost automatically assumed that the point of the play was in the literal story of the characters, and that Pirandello's new idea therefore was simply a new way to present the sordid tale. If so, then the play would be only another melodrama on the edge of psychopathology. It is this interpretation which Pirandello is at pains to reject first of all. "Now it must be understood that for me it is not enough to represent the figure of a man or a woman, however special or strongly marked, for the mere pleasure of representing it," he writes; "to tell a story (gay or sad) for the mere pleasure of telling it; to describe a landscape for the mere pleasure of describing it." When the story of the characters first occurred to him, it was in this realistic form; and as such it did not seem to him to be, as yet, the material of art, which must be "more philosophical than history." He was, in fact, through with modern realism: the literal scene, the actual individuals, and the sensational events of individual lives, no longer seemed to have any form or meaning. But when he sensed the analogy between his problem as an artist and the problems of his tormented characters who were also seeking form and meaning, he had the clue to his new theatrical form, and to the peculiar sense of human action (as itself theatrical) which this form was to realize. His inspiration was to stop the film of his characters' lives; to play over and over again some crucial episode in this sequence; to dispute its form and meaning on the public stage. By this means he found a mode of action which he, and the actors, and the characters, and the audience could all share by analogy, and which could thus be the clue to formal relationships and a temporal order. And he lifted the action, as it were, from the realm of fact and sensation, of eavesdropping and the curious intrigue, to the more disinterested realm of contemplation. "Always on opening the book we shall find the living Francesca confessing her sweet sin to Dante," Pirandello explains; "and if we return a hundred thousand times in succession to reread that passage, a hundred thousand times in succession Francesca will utter words, never repeating them mechanically, but speaking them every time for the first time with such a living and unforeseen passion that Dante, each time, will swoon when he hears them. Everything that lives, by the very fact that it lives, has form, and by that same fact must die; except the work of art, which precisely lives forever, in so far as it is form." Francesca's life, as developing potentiality, is stopped at the moment when her peculiar destiny is realized. And it is the crucial moments in the tangled lives of his characters—the moment in Pace's dress-shop, the pistol-shot in the garden—which must be played over with the vitality of improvisation, "as though for the first time," yet because they are played *over,* lifted to the realm of contemplation—it is these moments which the characters must interrogate in the light of the stage, as we all must mull over (though in secret) the moments when our nature and destiny are defined.

I have explained that Chekhov, in his way, also to some degree transcended the limits of modern realism: by selecting only those moments of the characters' lives, to show on-stage, when they are most detached from the literal facts and the stultifying rationalizations of the daily struggle. But in Chekhov these moments are suffered in abstraction from thought and purpose, and so his image of human action may seem too pathetic. He lacks both Ibsen's powerful moral-intellectual will and Shaw's fitness-in-the-void. But Pirandello, by means of his fiction of unwritten characters, can show the human creature both as suffering and as willfully endeavoring to impose his rationalization. This fiction-of-fictive-characters enables him to play over his catastrophes; and it was this resource which the realistic stage denied to Ibsen. When his Mrs. Alving, in *Ghosts,* suddenly sees Oswald's infatuation with Regina as a return of her husband's infatuation with Regina's mother, she gets the passionate but disinterested intuition which is the material of art, and is rewarded with the poetic vision that "we are *all* ghosts." But her final catastrophe—Oswald's collapse—strikes her for the first time only, and so remains, when the curtain falls, undigested and sensational. Pirandello's inspiration is to stop the action with Mrs. Alving's scream, and to play it over, in the actual light of the stage, the imagined lamp- and dawn-light of Mrs. Alving's parlor, and the metaphysical light of her, and our, need for some form and meaning.

Pirandello is at pains to explain, in his preface, that his play transcends not only modern realism, but also the various romantic genres with which some critics had confused it. The characters may be romantic, he says, but the play is not. The Daughter, for instance, when she takes the stage with her song, her deep feeling, and her abandoned charm, would like to seduce us into her own world of passion, as "the old magician Wagner" does in *Tristan.* But the scene is the stage itself, not her inner world; and her action meets perforce the actions of other characters who also claim the stage. Pirandello might also have said, with equal correctness, that his play transcends the Shavian irony, and at the same time realizes the farce of rationalizing with a depth and a consistency beyond that of Shaw. The Father, for instance, has a taste for the paradoxical platform, the unresolved ambiguity, and the logical consistency on the irrational premise, which reminds one strongly of Shaw. But he is present as a "real Character" first, and a rationalized platform second; hence we can believe in his sufferings as well as in his conceptualizing—and see both in a scene wider than either. The basis in reality of the Shavian farce appears, at last, to be in Shaw's own "gift" of abstract fitness and verbal agility; but Pirandello, in the stage itself and in our need not only to rationalize but to mythicize, has found a wider basis, on which many versions of human action may be shown together to the eye of contemplation.

There would be much to say of the extraordinary theatrical fertility of Pirandello's plot. The basic situation—the characters claiming the stage for their incommensurable tragic epiphanies, the actors claiming it for the marketable entertainment they are trying to make—has both comic and tragic aspects, and Pirandello exploits both, shifting from one to the other with perfect mastery. The situation, fictive though it admittedly is, has the firmness and clarity, once we have accepted it, of Racinian tragedy or Molièresque comedy. And just because it is so firm and unmistakable there is great freedom within it: it may be explored and developed with the apparent spontaneity of circus-clowning, the alertness and endless surprises of the Commedia Dell'Arte, where the actors improvised a performance on the broad clear basis of the plots of Latin comedy. The scenes may break into confusion—into philosophical arias and disputes; into laughter; into violence—but we are never lost. The stage, and the need to take the stage, frame the action as a mirror might, which no amount of grimacing can destroy—or like the *ampulla* in which the sibyl hangs, wishing to die, in the epigraph to *The Waste Land*. It is the static quality of this basic situation which is both its triumph and its limitation; and in order to understand it more fully, one must also think of some of its limitations.

I have remarked that the play is always breaking down in disputes about the idea and the reality or, more generally, art and life. It is in these issueless disputes that the Pirandellesque brilliance most closely resembles the Shavian brilliance; and indeed the unresolvable paradox on which they are based is like the basis of the "free" Shavian irony. But Pirandello, unlike Shaw, transcends his paradoxes by accepting them as final—or rather (since he does not, like Shaw, see human action as rationalizing only, and the world as merely conceptualized) he accepts his paradoxes as various versions of a final split in human nature and destiny itself. In the same way Racine, accepting the split between reason and passion as final, thereby transcends it: i.e., transforms it into an object of contemplation. Pirandello's version of this tragic contradiction (after the endless explorations of modern realism and romanticism) is more general than Racine's, and his concept of art is (after modern idealism) deeper and wider than Racine's *raison,* which corresponds to it. Pirandello's utter darkness of unformed Life (or *elan vital,* or *Wille,* or libido) is perhaps even more savage and less human than Racine's passion. Pirandello is not limited, like Racine, to the rigid scene of the enlightened moral will; he can present characters of various degrees of heroism and enlightenment; and, as I have remarked, he can accept and exploit the comic as well as the tragic aspects of his basic contradiction. Nevertheless, his tragedy is a limited, an invented, an artificial tragedy, on the same principle as Racine's; and in the same way it offers to the eye of the mind the eternity of the perfect, and perfectly tragic artifact—the human damned in his realization—instead of the transcendence of the tragic rhythm, which eschews the final clarity and leaves the human both real and mysterious.

One may also understand the limitations of Pirandello's theater by thinking again of its relation to modern realism. I have said that he "inverts" the scene of modern realism, and thus vastly increases the suggestiveness and the possible scope of the stage itself. But of course he does not, by this device, provide the chaotic modern world with a "theater" of action in the ancient sense. One might justly say that his attitude is more "realistic"—more disillusioned and disbelieving—than simple-minded positivism itself, for he does not have to believe in the photograph of the parlor, and he can accept the actual stage for the two boards it is. But he is left, like Ibsen and Chekhov, with neither an artistic convention like the Baroque, nor a stable scene of human life like the Greek or Elizabethan cosmos; and, like Ibsen and Chekhov, he has only the plot as a means of defining his action. The inspiration of *Six Characters* is thus not only the view of action as theatrical but the plot-device whereby this vision may be realized: the brilliant notion of making his protagonists unwritten "characters" and setting them to invade a stage. This plot is so right, so perfect, that it almost exhausts, and certainly obscures, the deeper insights into life and the theater which it realizes. Hence the natural though unjustified tendency to think of the play as a brilliant plot idea, a piece of theatrical trickery only, and so miss its deep and serious content. The complete dependence of the play upon its plot-idea constitutes a limitation; but it points to the fundamental problem of the modern theater, which no individual can solve alone.

Pirandello was quite right to think of his characters as being like Dante's Francesca. They too are caught and confined in the timeless moment of realizing their individual nature and destiny, and so imprisoned, damned, as she is. This vision has great authority. It develops naturally out of several diverse versions of the modern theater which I have mentioned, those of Ibsen, Wagner, and Shaw. At the same time it is deeply rooted in the Italian temperament and natural theatricality; and it revives crucial elements in the great theater of the Baroque. It is close to the author's place and to his times, which we share; yet one must remember that it takes as all-inclusive, as the whole story of human nature and destiny, a mode of action and understanding which Dante thought of as maimed, and which he presented in the realm of those who have lost, not the intellect, but the good of the intellect: *il ben dello intelletto.*

The most fertile property of Pirandello's dramaturgy is his use of the stage itself. By so boldly accepting it for what it is, he freed it from the demand which modern realism had made of it, that it be a literal copy of scenes off-stage, and also from the exorbitant Wagnerian demand, that it be an absolutely obedient instrument of hypnosis in the power of the artist. Thus he brought to light once more the wonderful property which the stage does have: of defining the primitive and subtle medium of the dramatic art. "After Pirandello"—to take him symbolically rather than chronologically—the way was open for Yeats and Lorca, Cocteau and Eliot. The search could start once more for a modern poetry of the theater, and even perhaps for an idea of the theater comparable to that of the Greeks yet tenable in the modern world.

ERIC BENTLEY

Enrico IV: *The Tragic Emperor*

A young man loves a woman and is not loved in return. What is more, he has a rival. In a costumed cavalcade, the rival causes the young man's horse to slip, and the young man falls, faints, and, when he comes to, is the victim of the delusion that he *is* the person whose costume he is wearing: the German Emperor Henry IV. His sister converts a villa into a replica of this Emperor's palace so that the young man can live on as Henry IV undisturbed. After twelve years, however, the delusion wears off. Our man, no longer so young, decides not to let anyone know it and to stay on as Emperor, though sane.

After eight more years, his sister dies. But she had visited him shortly before her death and gained the impression that he might now be curable. She tells her nephew this, and soon after her death he brings a psychiatrist to the villa to see what can be done. The psychiatrist, noticing on the wall portraits of our Emperor and the girl he loved, dating back to the time of the cavalcade, proposes a very precise form of shock treatment. He replaces the canvases by living human beings dressed up like the portraits. They make good likenesses, as one is the woman's own daughter, the other is the "Emperor's" nephew. The Doctor next makes the woman herself dress like the portrait. The idea is that the Emperor will notice that the pictures have come alive, then he will see the older woman, then he will look at himself, and noting in shock the difference between the older couple and the younger will be forced out of his illusion of having remained young, of having remained Henry IV.

From *Tulane Drama Review* 10, no. 3 (Spring 1966). © 1966 by *Tulane Drama Review*.

The Doctor's plan is of course bound to go wrong, since "Henry IV" has known for eight years that he is not Henry IV. Indeed, everyone else finds this out now from his attendants, to whom he has just released the secret. No sooner has he had an instant to receive the image of the two couples than in rushes everyone to announce the truth and confound confusion. But if the incident cannot have the effect on Henry that the Doctor intended, it does have an effect, and the Doctor's first impression is that it has reactivated the insanity, for Henry seems to accept the younger woman as the elder one, and later on tries to define the whole new situation in terms of this illusion, finally taking the girl in his arms. Her mother's lover—Henry's old rival— protests on the grounds that Henry is sane and able to control himself. "Sane, am I?" says Henry, and kills him on the spot.

That is the story of Luigi Pirandello's *Enrico IV,* and there is a temptation to think of the play as just these incidents with a good many little philosophical essays added. Some of the translations read that way, and Pirandello himself must bear the responsibility for some bad storytelling. The exposition is heavy and overcrowded, as maybe Pirandello realized when he wrote the stage direction that instructs the actors to play it vivaciously. Even the climactic scene of the play is badly articulated, for it is not just that Henry hasn't time to take in what is happening over the portraits—the audience hasn't time either.

Confusion here is presented confusingly, as indeed it is in the whole parallel between the modern young man and the Emperor Henry. One could wish that this Emperor were a man some conceivable audience would know about, so that they could recognize any parallels without effort or, failing this, that the story of the Emperor were so simple that the dramatist could put it across along with his modern plot. The very linking of the two stories certainly makes us assume a point-for-point parallel, but this expectation is disappointed, and bafflement results when, for example, while we see only two women on stage (Matilda, Frida) we are asked to imagine four in the life of the Emperor (Matilda, Agnes, Adelaide, Bertha). Nor—to follow through with the same example—do the modern pair always represent the same two medieval ladies. While one medieval figure (Matilda of Tuscany) is represented by both modern women, one of the modern women (Countess Matilda) represents two medieval women (Matilda of Tuscany, Duchess Adelaide). Some Pirandellians may wish to argue that this is the complexity of deliberate legerdemain and is meant to be bewildering, but others may be permitted to wonder how they can be expected to know this. If one is bewildered as to what is going on, must one not also be bewildered as to the author's intentions?

The question with a work of art that is notably obscure is whether the first puzzling acquaintance one had with it afforded such a premium of pleasure that one wishes to come back for more. In the case of *Enrico IV* there can surely be little doubt. At first encounter, it is hard to get the facts straight—and therefore impossible to get the meaning straight—but there is no doubt of the powerful impression made by the principal images, speeches, and scenes. The general scheme is itself very striking for anyone with the slightest predilection for Gothic fiction, and there are moments of exquisite theatrical poetry—such as the moment in which Henry dictates his life story to Giovanni—which make their mark even before we ask questions about the main drift.

When we do come to these questions, the first question of all is inevitably: what about this German Emperor? Why did it have to be him? I thought I might find some clues when I found mentioned by Benjamin Cremieux the titles of the books Pirandello had consulted on the subject: Voigt's life of Pope Gregory VII and Oncken's *Allgemeine Geschichte.* But I did not find much in these that seemed more to the purpose than an encyclopedia article on the subject unless it was two pictures—of the Abbey of Cluny and the palace at Goslar, respectively. Pirandello worked with the elementary facts of Henry's life as they might be related by any history teacher. Because Henry came to the throne as a mere child, his mother, Agnes, acted as Regent. She came under suspicion of adultery with the Bishop of Augsburg and had to be removed. To this bit of pure history Pirandello adds the fiction that the accusation of adultery was brought by an ecclesiastical friend of the Vatican's: Peter Damiani. Aside from this, all that is filled in of Henry's earlier life is that he had trouble keeping his German barons and ecclesiastics in line. Pirandello, like other people, is mainly interested in what happened when Henry was twenty-six; namely, his arch-enemy, the Pope, brought him literally to his knees and he knelt in the snow hoping that the Pope would give him an audience. His wife, the Empress Bertha, knelt with him, and Bertha's mother, Duchess Adelaide, went with the Abbot of Cluny, another friendly witness, to plead with the Pope and the latter's ally, Countess Matilda of Tuscany.

Here Pirandello adds something of more significance than the involvement of Peter Damiani. "I wanted," he has been quoted as saying, "a situation where a historical personage was in love with a woman who was his enemy." Not finding what he wanted, he created it. Matilda of Tuscany was indeed Henry IV's enemy, but no historian records that he loved her. Pirandello invents this motif, and lets us know it in the play itself by having Landolf remark that Henry secretly loves Matilda even though the historians say nothing about it. It is only through his own Matilda that Pirandello's nameless young protagonist comes to the Emperor Henry IV in the first place. The modern Matilda had already picked her medieval namesake as her role in the masquerade, and that is what gave her young man the idea of being Henry:

> I said I'd like to be Countess Matilda of Tuscany. . . . I just heard him saying, "Then I'll be at your feet at Canossa. . . . " I now understood why he wanted to be next to me in the cavalcade as the Emperor . . . because I'd chosen to represent his implacable enemy.

And because he secretly loved her. What the nameless young man finds in history besides a name and the status of an emperor is a relationship of love-hate.

Pirandello's Emperor seems most of the time stuck in his twenty-sixth year (1077), but he has some power to bob about in his private time machine, and is particularly concerned with the years 1076 and 1080. In 1076 at Tribur the German princes had proposed to depose Henry. His famous gesture at Canossa turns out on further scrutiny not to be a sincere and definitive submission before Papal authority but a sly man's effort to head off the prospect of facing his accusers. By 1080 Henry's position had been strengthened to the point where it was not *his* throne that was in danger but the Pope's own. This was an Emperor who, when the Pope was not to his liking, would set up another: the Henry of Pirandello's play prophesies that at Brixen he will declare Pope Gregory deposed. That the historical Emperor outlived by many years both Canossa and Brixen is acknowledged by Pirandello only in the statement that his life contained the material for many tragedies.

It would be a mistake to pursue the historical Henry past the point where Pirandello takes leave of him, or to hunt for more parallels than the play immediately suggests to anyone who knows the historical outline, for beyond this point history will become the play's rival and a victorious rival at that. By putting into the play itself the few historical facts he needs, the author is declaring the other facts off limits. After all, drawing upon some very suggestive incidents and relationships, he has created a plot and characters that are his own and not at all medieval. We perhaps need to brush aside the Gothic trappings altogether for a minute or two if we are to glimpse his characters as they are.

Pirandello is an Ibsenite dramatist. I have suggested elsewhere that for Ibsen man is neurotic and that for Pirandello man is even more deeply neurotic, is indeed never far enough from psychosis to be out of danger of falling into it. Has it been noticed how very far gone are all three of the main characters in *Enrico IV?* Pirandello's full awareness of what he was doing in this respect could be illustrated by the stage directions in which some of the characters—Dr. Genoni for instance—are first introduced. But stage directions stand outside the drama proper, and the dialogue itself is rich enough in evidence. Matilda's character, for instance, is defined in the following passage from act 1:

COUNTESS: . . . I *was* natural in those days. . . .

BARON: You see: she couldn't abide him!

COUNTESS: That's not true! I didn't even dislike him. Just the opposite! But with me, if a man wants to be taken seriously—

BARON: —he gives the clearest proof of his stupidity!

COUNTESS: Don't judge others by yourself, Baron. *He* wasn't stupid.

BARON: But then *I* never asked you to take me seriously.

COUNTESS: Don't I know it! But with him it was no joke. My dear Doctor, a woman has a sad life, a silly life. And some time or other it's her lot to see a man's eyes fixed upon her, steady and intense and full of—shall we say?—the promise of enduring sentiment? (*She bursts into a harsh laugh.*) What could be funnier? If only men could see their looks of enduring sentiment!—I've always laughed at them. More at *that* time than any other.—And let me tell you something: I can still laugh at them, after more than twenty years.— When I laughed like that at *him*, it was partly from fear, though. Perhaps one could have believed a promise in *those* eyes. It would've been dangerous, that's all.

DOCTOR: —Why dangerous?

COUNTESS (*with levity*): Because he wasn't like the others. And because I too am . . . I can't deny it . . . I'm a little . . . intolerant, that's the word. I don't like stuffiness, I don't like people who take life hard.—Anyway, I was too young at that time, you understand? And I was a woman: I couldn't help champing at the bit.—It would have needed courage, and I didn't have any.—So *I* laughed at him too. With remorse. With real self-hatred. . . .

The same conversation gives us all we need to know of the protagonist before he appears. People laughed at him behind his back:

DOCTOR: Ahem, yes, um . . . he was already rather strange . . .
exalted, as it were—if I've been following you properly?

BARON: Yes, but after a very curious fashion, Doctor . . . he was
damned cold-blooded about it—

COUNTESS: Cold-blooded? What nonsense! This is how it was,
Doctor. He was a little strange, it's true: that was because
there was so much life in him. It made him—eccentric.

BARON: . . . He was often genuinely exalted. But I could swear,
Doctor: he was looking at himself, looking at his own exaltation. And I believe the same is true of every move he made,
however spontaneous: he *saw* it. I'll say more: I'm certain it
was this that made him suffer. At times he had the funniest
fits of rage against himself . . . the lucidity that came from
acting all the time . . . being another man . . . shattered, yes,
shattered at a single blow, the ties that bound him to his own
feelings. And these feelings seemed—well, not exactly a pretense, no, they were sincere—but he felt he must give them
an intellectual status, an intellectual form of expression—to
make up for his lack of warmth and spontaneity—so he
improvised, exaggerated, let himself go, that's about it, to
deafen his own ears, to keep his eyes from seeing himself. He
seemed fickle, silly, and sometimes . . . yes, ridiculous, let's
face it.

Now drama is not made up of character sketches, nor even of characters
set side by side: character is rendered by relationships, and relationships are
defined in happenings. The happenings in Pirandello are not only collisions
(which would be true of much other drama), they are traumatic collisions.
His plays hinge on scenes that have the quality of haunting fantasies, like
the "primal scene" of psychoanalysis. *Enrico IV* is built upon several traumatic
moments. The moment when the protagonist fell from his horse comes first
to mind, but of equal weight is the moment, twelve years later, when he woke
up to know he was not the Emperor. Then there is the moment, eight years
after that, which is the occasion of the action presented on stage, the moment
when the other actors in the original drama dare to return to it after two
decades: such is act 1. The play moves on to two further traumatic moments:
the moment when the planned trauma does not take place, but another one
does, as the nameless hero sees the living portraits and the crowd rushes in
to say he is sane; and, secondly, the moment in which "Henry" murders
Belcredi.

How many readers will notice that the foregoing list omits the most important trauma of them all? I omitted it involuntarily by a kind of "Freudian" forgetting that somehow belongs.

> COUNTESS: . . . A woman has a sad life, a silly life. And some time or other it's her lot to see a man's eyes fixed upon her, steady and intense and full of—shall we say?—the promise of enduring sentiment? . . .

We know she is describing the unnamed one's love for her. He picks up the thread at the very climax of his eloquence in act 2.

> Woe betide you if, like me, you are swallowed up by a thought that will really drive you mad. You are with another human being, you're at their side, you look into their eyes—how well I remember doing it that day!—and you might as well be a beggar before some door you will never pass through!

In comparison with a murder, or a fall from a horse, the incident is small, but I call it the most important trauma of them all because without it the other traumas either would not have occurred or would have much less significance. At the heart of this Gothic quasi history, this Germanic quasi-philosophical treatise, is a Sicilian melodrama—or opera libretto, if you will—love, jealousy, and revenge. The culmination of such a melodrama is the death of the rival, and the first stage along the violent road to this destination was reached when the rival tripped the hero's horse. Pirandello's plays are variants on such patterns, and Pirandello is giving this particular pattern a new center when he brings the eyes of hero and heroine together, not in the expected exchange of love, but in the unexpected failure to exchange anything. The woman's eyes are a door the man will never pass through. This incident, this situation, undercuts the melodrama because, now, victory over one's rival is fruitless: love is not to be had anyhow. In this way, melodrama becomes drama "of the absurd," becomes "grotesque" in the sense Jan Kott uses the term when he states that in a grotesque work "both alternatives of the choice imposed are absurd, irrelevant, or compromising."

Kott is concerned not with melodrama but with tragedy. "What once was tragedy," he says, "today is grotesque." But this too is a thesis which *Enrico IV* exemplifies. The play has been described as Pirandello's one real tragedy, and in some Italian editions it is subtitled *Una Tragedia*. It is certainly Pirandello's *Hamlet*. Belcredi is its Claudius, Countess Matilda its Gertrude, Frida its Ophelia. And Hamlet's antic disposition has spread itself over the whole life of the Pirandellian protagonist.

There is *talk* of tragedy in the play. For if the nameless one has chosen to be Henry IV because the latter is the enemy of Matilda of Tuscany, he has chosen him equally because he was the *tragic* emperor, whose life indeed contained "material for many tragedies." (Henry IV is called *il tragico imperatore* in Pirandello's *Rhenish Elegies*.) His aim in life is nothing less than to attain to tragic seriousness, as he makes quite explicit in the speech about the priest who returns to his priestliness from the truancy of a frivolous dream. "Back into his eyes came the same seriousness that you have seen in mine, for Irish priests defend the seriousness of their Catholic faith with the same zeal I felt for the sacred rights of hereditary monarchy."

The protagonist insists on tragedy; the author does not. The protagonist is a character in search of the tragic poet: such is Pirandello's subject, which therefore comes out absurd, grotesque, tragicomic. "Comic" is the conventional opposite of "tragic," even as joking is the usual opposite of seriousness. In Pirandello's play, the protagonist's wish to be serious, to be taken seriously, stems from a feeling that he is *not* serious, that people do not take him seriously. This we are told at the outset, where Matilda speaks of "all the fools who made fun of him," after which Pirandello never lets the theme go. Is Enrico ridiculous, or isn't he? Are people laughing at him or aren't they? Are his actions jokes and jests or aren't they? The words "joke" and "jest" are reiterated obsessively, and always in connection with making a joke or jest of something that should *not* be joked or jested about. Matilda is, in this respect, the agent of the action, since she does, or has done, the laughing. And she has turned from the man she laughed at in fear to the man she laughs at in scorn. *Everything that happens in the whole bizarre series of events is a joke*, bad or good. The idea of the cavalcade was a joke. The tripping of the horse was a practical joke of Belcredi's. The original joke of the masquerade is perpetuated by the re-creation of the Goslar palace in an Umbrian villa. The action we see on stage is meant seriously by its in-stigators but is turned into a joke by others. The exposition is intended as farce (even if it does not quite work out that way). Genoni is a doctor out of Molière or Ben Jonson. His grand design is closer to *commedia dell'arte* than to the clinic, and Belcredi is there to make us aware of this. A high point in the action is reached when the nameless one reveals to the atten-dants that he is not mad. The conclusion they draw is that his life in the villa has been a jest. This interpretation produces "Henry's" first great burst of rage. His second, which ends the play, grows out of an act-long quarrel between Belcredi and himself about this matter of joking. "The whole thing was a joke . . . he put on an act so he could have a good laugh behind your back . . . let's have done with this perpetual jesting!" The attendants have told Belcredi the madness was a jest. Belcredi calls the masquerade a joke, and the nameless one counters with: "It wasn't such a joke to me as you think."

The ending of the play, which perhaps seems arbitrary when we detach it from the thematic structure, grows organically enough out of the perpetual torturesome question: Is anything more than a jest at stake? The effect of the Doctor's shock treatment is to make the nameless one review the whole situation, not of course in philosophic calm, but in the frenzy induced by the crisis. What he comes back to again and again is the danger of being ridiculous—of his tragedy being reduced to a comedy. Should he, now that he is cured, go out of doors and be a modern man? "To have everyone secretly pointing at me and whispering, Emperor Henry?" When Matilda says, "Who could even conceive of such a thing? An accident is an accident," the nameless one reaches back to the basic fact and premise of the whole fable: "They all said I was mad—even before—all of them!" To this Belcredi retorts: "That was only a joke!" He thinks the retort will make matters better: it makes them much worse since the question of frivolity is even more crucial than that of sanity. The nameless one angrily shows his grey hair. Is that a joke? Then he comes out with the true story of how his horse was tripped. "That must have been a joke too!" Then he defines his own general position as a transcendance of jokes: "not a jest, no, a reality." "And one walks around—a tragic character." Thence to the main situation of the last act, the re-creation of the young Matilda in her daughter Frida. "To me it could hardly be the joke they intended, it could only be this terrible prodigy: a dream come alive." He embraces the living dream. Belcredi cannot believe he is "serious" and protests. Not serious? Not serious? How can the jealous rival prove he is not joking, not play-acting? By using a real sword and producing a real death. In this way the nameless one preserves his image of himself as tragic hero, while Pirandello, by the same stroke, decisively detaches his play from tragedy. For, after all, what our hero has just done *is* crazy, *is* ridiculous, and objectively he has tragic dignity just as little as other lunatics who pose as emperors.

In distinguishing between the protagonist's image of himself and Pirandello's image of him, I am declining to take the play as a *pièce à thèse* in which the hero is the author's mouthpiece. It is true he often gives voice to sentiments concerning illusion and reality which we at once spot as Pirandellian commonplaces. Taken as *pièce à thèse, Enrico IV* is very neat indeed. It says that "Henry" was all right till these interlopers came to try and cure him. He was all right both in having recovered from insanity and in having found a solution that is even better than sanity: the conscious acceptance of illusion as a way of life. What the interlopers do bids fair to cancel the solution but "Henry" preserves it and perpetuates it the only way he can. The final murder, thus understood, comes to us simply as a logical conclusion and we respond not with a gasp of horror but with a nod of the head—Q.E.D. Similarly, we have to take the play as wholly abstract: we cannot for a moment take the characters as men and women and ask questions like: What kind of person commits a murder of this kind? What would you make of a murder like this if it happened in your own family circle?

Such an approach overlooks what Pirandello has himself put into this play. Though his "Henry" woos and perhaps wins us with his magnificent speeches about illusion and reality, the action of the play does not confirm Henry's theories (i.e., his hopes). What does he actually conclude when he finds himself sane? That so long as the others do not *know* him to be sane, they will provide him with an unusual privilege: that of living in a dream world for the fun of it with the support of all one's friends. Normally one's friends exact a price: they require that one be really insane. So Henry's opportunity was unique! One's first impulse is to call what he is doing "Living the illusion but being the only one to see through it." But of course the others see through it too. They only don't know that he does. So what we have is a compact based on a misunderstanding created by a benevolent deception. This compact generates a certain amount of good. It would therefore be bad to threaten it. But, on the other hand, it has not produced a little Utopia, not even an ideal state of affairs for a single man. For "Henry's" scheme, in its highest flights, does not work. He would like to insert himself into the eleventh century and simply "be." The pleasure of history, as he expounds it, is to be Henry IV forever. But he is confused as to just how to achieve this. It could mean that he is forever Henry IV at the moment of Canossa, in which case he will always be twenty-six years old. Or it could mean that he is free to move up and down the whole life of Henry IV, enjoying the fact that what happens is already settled and one need not live in uncertainty. The confusion here, clearly enough rendered by Pirandello, is not that of a theory but of a man—a madman.

On whose authority do we have it that the nameless one was ever cured? Only his own. But will not many a psychotic claim to be well? It is perhaps curious how easily readers of Pirandello accept Henry's own claims. They could say that, in a degree, Henry offers proof that what he says is true: *He* knows he isn't really a German Emperor, and *we* know he isn't really a German Emperor. But is merely the absence of this delusion a proof of sanity? At this point we may well bog down in semantic difficulties. What *is* sanity? It is Pirandello himself, however, who makes us aware of this danger. His punning on the word makes us ask finally if *sanity* is any more *sane* than *insanity.* But without looking for a solution of the semantic problem, can we not go on to say that, sane or insane, the protagonist of *Enrico IV* is presented as a deeply disturbed person? And by "presented" we mean "presented to our eyes and ears"; we are not talking of his mental health eight years earlier. In fact, I have already quoted the passages in which it is heavily underlined that "Henry" had been conspicuously abnormal from the beginning. Is it not perverse, then, to see the murder he commits as a merely symbolic affair? Murder is a serious business, committed in massive rage that has had much time and much reason to accumulate: only thus, generally speaking, can we find it credible. But just such factors are present in the play. The murder (*pace* the semanticists) itself seems crazy. And the rhythm of the action seems to derive from the reactivization of the nameless one's trouble through the incidents we witness. This reactivization is prepared dramatically as early as act 1. What is going on inside "Henry" in that act can scarcely be judged on first reading or seeing: there are too many surprises to take in and one doesn't know what to look for. But then first acts in general are to be appreciated at *second* reading. At such a second reading this first act hardly gives the impression of a sane "Henry," even if we make allowance for deliberate whimsy and playfulness on his part.

Let anyone who thinks the nameless one has constructed a foolproof illusion consider what its major premise is: that time can be stopped. "Henry" *has* stopped time to the extent that he can stay in the eleventh century and never need to jump to the twentieth. Even this, however, he achieved only when he actually thought he was the Emperor: when the twelve years were up he knew exactly which century he was in. As to stopping time in the more vital sense that his own body should stay the same age, the nameless one has no illusions: his gray hairs tell him all. And in exploring Pirandello's handling of the point we learn not only that *he* had no illusions either, but that he handled the matter dialectically and brought it to a conclusion not only different from popular "Pirandellianism" but diametrically opposite to it. His hero tried to go on being the twenty-six-year-old German Emperor, yet not only could not build himself a heaven in fantasy, but longed for the other life, the twentieth-century one, that he was missing. Pirandello audaciously places Henry's confession of this at the end of act 1. Is it contradicted by the fact that when later the doors are opened, and the nameless one could go out in the modern world, he refuses? It is; but the contradiction is that of his character and of a universal human situation. True, he has an alibi: it is too late. But when would it not have been too late? Is this a melodrama in which a healthy Innocent has been deprived of his rights by the Villainous Belcredi? At some moments, *he* can think so; but not at all. And at no moment can *we* think so. This is a story of a life not lived in a world of people incapable of living.

Has the fantasy, then, no positive content at all? It has. Here again the thinking is two-sided and dialetical. "Henry" has found himself a *modus vivendi*, and it is true that the visit of the Doctor and the others destroys this (until he builds up again on another foundation), but the *modus vivendi* was itself imperfect, flawed, full of tragicomic conflict caused by two factors already suggested: the impossibility of the main endeavor (stopping time) and, secondly, the precariousness of the structure of deception and misunderstanding (sooner or later the happy accidents must have an end). It follows that Pirandello's own vision—as distinct from that of some of his Pirandellian spokesmen—is not just of illusion within illusion: there are nonillusions here. Or, stating this differently, illusions are finally only illusions, and one sees through them. It is, on the other hand, no illusion that the nameless one's hair turned gray; or that Belcredi, at the end, is dead as a doornail.

The illusions which many harbor about Pirandello's illusionism come perhaps from assuming that his plays are *about* the philosophy, an assumption it was easy to make when the philosophy was novel and shocking. What is such a play as *Enrico IV* really about? What is at the center of Pirandello's interest, and hence of his play? Necessarily, since he is a major playwright, not a philosopher, what is at the center will not be opinion as such but experience. What he gives us is in fact the *experience* of a man with Pirandellian *opinions,* a man who has applied himself to the Pirandellian task of "constructing himself." That was the meaning of his "play-acting" even in advance of the masquerade. That was the meaning of the masquerade itself and, involuntarily, of the insanity afterward. The point is that "Henry" *always failed.* We even learn in the last act that while he was Emperor (presumably in the "insane period") he noticed his hair turning gray—noticed, that is, that the whole scheme had broken down. In the later phase in which we encounter him on stage he claims to find a solution in *being aware* that one is only an actor in a masquerade, which is preferable, he says, to being such an actor without knowing it. But the play does not show that it really makes much difference whether one is aware of such things or not. Certainly, the four attendants don't "buy" the idea. The one happy human moment of the play, that between "Henry" and Giovanni, is created, significantly enough, by a misunderstanding: Giovanni thinks "Henry" is still mad. And the last act would seem to say that sooner or later any construct is destroyed by life itself.

If the play as a whole embodies a philosophy, that philosophy is pessimistic and materialist, where "Henry" is an optimist and idealist. Just think how this Hamlet-parody differs from *Hamlet* in its last act. Claudius *has* to be killed: heaven itself has said so. And if there is foul play in the killing, Claudius himself is responsible. In *Enrico,* the murder is itself foul play, a vicious and shabby act: a swordsman stabs an unarmed man in the belly. Was Pirandello remembering Eilert Løvborg's failure to shoot himself in the head? At all events, the belly is the least heroic of close-range targets. The thought makes Henry's presumed heroic image of himself all the more fantastic. The note that is struck here is of course the modern one. This is not tragedy, a heroic genre, but post-Dostoevski psychological drama showing the decline and fall of a man through mental sickness to crime.

Are Pirandello's plays more about reality and illusion than they are about love and absence of love? The search for truth is generally conducted by the trivial and bad people in them, while the more serious people seek love. It may be said that the latter often declare love to be unattainable. But what relief there is in seeming to discover the undiscoverability of what one is all the time seeking! Yet love is not inherently impossible to the people Pirandello presents. It has only *become* impossible—and for psychological, not metaphysical, reasons. The whole of *Enrico IV* lies in germ in Belcredi's original description of the nameless one (already quoted) as a man suffering from a strange exaltation and always watching his own exalted state, a sufferer who had fits of rage against himself, an actor who, through acting so much, lost touch with himself, a man who lacked spontaneous warmth, and who, to make up for this, improvised and play-acted to the point of the ridiculous. The same part of act 1 lets us see that self-hatred and self-abasement are a sort of family neurosis in which all three main characters are sunk. Here surely we find Pirandello's ultimate reason for lighting on the Canossa story: the Emperor Henry IV has fixed only one thing in the memory of the world, his act of self-abasement before the Pope. All the more interesting, of course, if this Emperor's gesture proves, upon closer examination, to have had low cunning in it. We then realize all the more vividly that there was no humility in the action: it was ignoble through and through.

"In stories like this," says the Gardener in Giraudoux's *Electra,* "the people won't stop killing and biting each other to tell you the one aim of life is to love." Here, too, is the modern note: love can be all inference, while what is exhibited is lovelessness and hate. So with Pirandello, love is absent; present are self-hatred, self-abasement, self-mockery. The "loss of self" here is not mere absence of self, let alone a mere theory that there *is* no self, it is an assault on the self by the self. At the psychological center of this play is psychic masochism brilliantly suggested at the outset by the nagging, irritable, sarcastic tone in which Belcredi and Matilda address each other. The nameless one's final assault upon himself takes the form of murder. While from the viewpoint of "Pirandellianism" the murder of Belcredi may seem laudable, within the world created by Pirandello in his play it is but the final culmination of this masochism and is to be construed (like most murders, after all) as the ultimate measure taken by the murderer against himself.

If this sounds grandiose, I would suggest that, on the contrary, the present line of thought permits one to speak more "realistically" (i.e. literal-mindedly) about both the play and its protagonist. It is the story of an orphan whose orphanhood has been compounded by insanity and incarceration. We meet him at a time that is especially unfortunate even for a man of many misfortunes. The sister who had been something of a mother to him has just died. This great loss is duplicated on a more trivial scale by the loss of the servant Tony who had played the role of Bishop of Bremen. While he is suffering intensely from the pains of deprivation (just such pains as are responsible for the mental trouble in *Right You Are,* incidentally) the nameless one is arbitrarily confronted with the one woman he has ever loved and the man who stole her from him by the trick which made him a madman. As if these factors would not be enough to produce an explosion, Dr. Genoni then adds his preposterous plot. Genoni's drama did not show the nameless one that he was irretrievably cut off now from Youth as shown in the portraits. It brought to life the portrait of the Loved One and thus seemed to offer the nameless one all he had ever wanted: Matilda when young. At no point is it brought home to us more vividly than here how aware "Henry" has really become of the loss of both Matilda and his youth. Otherwise he would not be so struck by this living image which he knows is not really Matilda. He is not "taken in," but he is overwhelmed with feeling, and, when Belcredi intervenes, the irritability which would be the normal response has reason to be multiplied a hundred-fold in a rage that means murder. Illusions are falling before realities, right and left. And the conclusion is renewed illusion? Not exactly. There will be a pretense of it, that is all: an illusion of illusion. The reality is that the nameless one, already parentless, childless, brotherless before the "play" started, has now lost the Attendants as far as their old roles are concerned, and has reduced himself to an ultimate misery. Not only can he no longer dream of being cut loose from his Emperor, he cannot even live as Emperor either, for the Attendants no longer believe him mad. At the end he is as "cabined, cribbed, confined" as a Beckett character up to the waist in earth or up to the neck in a jar.

DANTE DELLA TERZA

On Pirandello's Humorism

The events that brought Luigi Pirandello to write his essay "L'umorismo" in 1908 are on the whole well known. After fifteen years of a career reluctantly spent teaching stylistics in a girls' college in Rome, he needed a solid publication in order to convince his judging peers of the seriousness of his academic involvement. And indeed, the essay that enabled him to earn a tenured position in his school has all the connotations of a scholarly endeavor. By calling to task the authorities on humorism—D'Ancona, Bonghi, and Nencioni for Italy, Taine for France, and his own former teacher in Bonn, Theodor Lipps, for Germany—Pirandello in fact shows an impeccable knowledge of the discussions on the subject; by differentiating his point of view from the opinions of others with the caution of a self-restrained scholar, he indicates that he knows how to avoid the risk of transforming his intellectual assets, of which his colleagues in Italy were certainly well aware, into a professional liability.

As is all too obvious, however, if the academic pressure could in a certain way condition the length of the essay, or the thickness of its erudite apparatus, it nevertheless appears immaterial or bears only marginal significance when we come to explain the deep motivation of Pirandello's undertaking. Even the dedication, to "the late Mattia Pascal, librarian"— that is, to a figment of Pirandello's imagination, to the most eloquent fictional mouthpiece of his relativism—strikes a dissonant note irrelevant to and contrasting with the erudite purpose of the essay.

A careful look at the material that constitutes the bulk of the essay shows,

From *Veins of Humor* (Harvard English Studies 3), edited by Harry Levin. © 1972 by the President and Fellows of Harvard College. Harvard University Press, 1972.

furthermore, that Pirandello's reading in the works of literature related to humorism only represents a frame of reference called upon to support a highly personal order of values toward which the critical discourse is impatiently gravitating. The works of Pulci, Rabelais, Ariosto, and Cervantes—unavoidable topics for an essay on humorism—act as an impressive reservoir of learned examples and constitute above all a vehicle of clarification for a theoretical issue that bears particular force for Pirandello the artist. In fact, while preparing his essay, Pirandello had already ceased to believe in knowledge as a goal to be reached through daily efforts, a goal having in itself its torments and its rewards. Rather, he considered it a heritage to be absorbed in the focus of a vision eternally present for the spirit of the artist, in an all-consuming act of creation. As early as the beginning of the century, Pirandello's culture was fixed and crystallized: a product of an enthusiastic experience to be placed in his German years, when he considered himself basically a linguist and a romance philologist, hence in the past. Thus in a sense in the essay on humorism, not only the exemplifications, but the images themselves—even the most striking ones, in spite of their appearance of genial improvisation—are recurrent experiences returning to the page with almost formulaic value to prove what has already been proven, to underline the *déjà vu:* at once focus of repose and obsessive fixity.

It is the merit of one of the first reviewers of Pirandello's essay, Benedetto Croce, to have realized the marginality of its erudite apparatus and to have discarded that altogether from his critical considerations. By showing little or no concern for the diachronical disposition of Pirandello's material, Croce at first seems inclined to emphasize that in the matter of humorism only theoretical assumptions have the right to be considered relevant, and that Pirandello's conceptualization of art should not so much be judged in its historical application to authors whom he happens to call humorists as it should be evaluated in itself, by going at the very roots of its esthetic relevance. No wonder then if, in agreement with a monistic conception of art that allows no classification of sentiments, no reflective mood capable of defeating the free expansion of the artist's imagination, Croce dismisses Pirandello's effort as theoretically unsound. The counteracting reflexes of Pirandello's humorist, always looking at the other side of the coin, freezing his initial thrust for life or reversing it in negation of life, could only appear to Croce as the product of a sincerely tormented but chaotic mind, and at best as the offspring of the moody improvisation of a philosophizing dilettante.

It should however be added that—since for Croce an erroneous ideology of knowledge does not necessarily create a false form of art, the creating artist in the depths of his imagination being able to reach for compensating resources unknown to the artist as a theoretician and unforeseen by him—it may well happen that in the matter of Pirandello's humorism Croce's primary target is not necessarily what it appears to be. In fact his opposition to the cognitive effort of Pirandello's mind ought to be definitely placed within the framework of his inborn distrust of any artistic vision of the world, from Leopardi's *Operette morali* to Pirandello's theater, that is imbued with an irredeemably pessimistic outlook.

As for Pirandello, though in disagreement with Croce on practically everything, he accepts the assumption that the source of art is imaginative and not conceptual. Paradoxically, however, humorism, the only form of art in which he is truly interested, is also to him the only one ready to open the door of the creative process to reflection. All his efforts, when talking of humorism, are therefore turned to justifying that exceptional experience which humorism underlines, without denying the truth of the above-mentioned statement concerning the imaginative nature of artistic expression.

Pirandello's definition of humorism as *sentimento del contrario* indicates a dilemma at the core of his aesthetic convictions. If *sentimento del contrario* does not mean, as in my opinion it does not, the objective manifestation of a challenging emotion, counteracting from the opposite pole the expansion of another emotion obstructing its path—if it is not the vectorial force carrying the rights of an emotion well into the alien territory of an opposite emotion which has acquired undue prominence—it could only indicate the presence of a subjective "feeling" that somewhere in the stratified world of our affections there is an emotional explosion that shakes our privileged heritage of sentiments, refusing to accept them as the only ones which really "are." This "feeling," however, is not really a kind of seismograph limiting itself to measuring the waves of an emotional earthquake, in spite of the qualifications attributed to it by Pirandello; it is not a sentiment at all, since its activity is overwhelmingly critical, analytical, and rational. By trying to give another name to a cognitive activity Pirandello, instead of making his dilemma inconspicuous, as he would have liked, ends up by giving the limelight, unwittingly but revealingly, to an all-encompassing and proliferating imagery suggested by the intrusive concept of reflection.

In order to qualify better the issue of reflection versus sentiment, I shall quote a few examples of what I would like to call the metamorphic presence of reflection in the core of Pirandello's essay on humorism. Reflection appears at first in the guise of a judge who calls the artist to duty and meanwhile helps him to decompose a given sentiment. It may well be that by analyzing and decomposing a sentiment or its image, this demiurgic and personified reflection literally creates the counteracting sentiment, which freezes the expansion of the previous one or at least erodes its territory. There is of course a significant difference between "creating" an emotion almost *ex nihilo,* or at least unpredictably through the manipulation of another emotion, and acknowledging its presence in the bulk of reality, or detecting its objective right to exist as a negation and reversal of the truths more obviously established. The dividing line between idealistic subjectivism—also in its relativistic impact—and positivistic objectivism is, in Pirandello, far from easy to trace. A connotative sign of the detachment and objectivity in the judging role attributed to reflection can be detected in the emphasis Pirandello gives to a kind of philosophical remoteness attainable by looking through turned-around binoculars at the surrounding human landscape.

Reflection also appears in the deceitful form of a mirror composed of iced waters in which the flame of the sentiment dives to extinction. The fizzling of the water and the steam coming from the liquid surface become, for Pirandello, alluring symbols for the laugh aroused by the humorist and for his somewhat smoky imagination. This is the point at which Pirandello comes closest to an imagistic definition of humorism. The same result is envisioned when Pirandello rather obscurely underlines the equivalence of reflection and a malignant wild plant: the mistletoe, which grows about the seed of a pre-existing sentiment in order to awaken ideas and images in contrast with it, thus transforming it.

The laboriously analogical equivalents for humorism—strident laugh, aerial trace of smoke, and malignant wild mistletoe provoking the metamorphosis of a seed—succeed better in describing the erosive power of reflection over a given sentiment than in helping us figure out its activity in positively creating antagonistic and challenging images (the so-called *sentimenti del contrario*) in the humoristic work of art. Such a function is more efficiently taken up by a different set of statements through which Pirandello, though initially seduced by the usual complicated series of analogies, finally abandons his camouflage of metaphors and reaches the ground of historical reality.

"The spider of experience," Pirandello writes in "L'umorismo," "abstracts from social life the silk floss in order to compose in the individual the web of opinions in which the moral sense often lies enveloped. Since social relations are often nothing but a calculation in which morality is sacrificed, the task of humorism is that of discovering, through a laugh and without indignation, hypocrisy behind morality."

A close analysis of the preceding paragraph, if we are able to elude the pitfalls created by overstretched metaphors and syntactic intricacies, could lead us to see more clearly the link existing between Pirandello's theoretical statements on humorism and his concrete experimentations as an artist.

It is, for instance, to be noted that on the one hand the individual, almost surreptitiously introduced into the core of the sentence, does not act but is acted upon; on the other hand the spider of experience—the grammatical subject—in spite of its obtrusiveness, remains as abstract as its already discussed vegetal equivalent, the mistletoe of reflection. We have thus—in its full expansion, but completely disembodied from its human support—an idea that, having acquired an abnormal body, moves to entangle the individual in its web.

But in Pirandello the silk thread is a material the spider of experience derives from society. What we have here, carried through the ambiguous byways of metaphor expressing a kind of physiological repulsion on the part of the author, is the paradigm of a basic conflict between society, with its rituals of oppression and hypocrisy, and the individual trapped in them to his own detriment and destruction. Before reaching the elusive but real ground of this uneven struggle, the humorist instinctively establishes an ambivalent link with the conflict he is denouncing. The ingredients of this relationship are manifold: at the level of the subconscious we have already acknowledged the writer's repulsion for the omnivorous spider abstracting its web from society to suffocate the individual's freedom to act. On a more conscious and evident level, the writer's laugh reveals the many degrees of his participation in the drama of human existence. By expressing awareness of foul play hidden behind dissimulation and hypocrisy it shows, according to rules established by Thomas Hobbes in his essay on human nature, the writer's superiority over the terms of the conflict. By denying him any room for indignation, this very laugh paves the way for an all-encompassing and equidistant understanding involving the victim with his hypocritical oppressor. And still—putting aside the very special issues discussed later in this paper in which the author, through his mouthpiece, takes a privileged role in the fiction or play—in most cases Pirandello as a writer never stands above or aside from the conflict as a detached witness. Rather, he works from within, demiurgically precipitating a confrontation deprived of intermediaries between the oppressing society and the undaunted individual.

At the end of these remarks on the essay on humorism, it should be asked how the narrative theory such an essay espouses, which is based on the demiurgic interference of the writer with the false rationale of human motivations, could be preceded by the period of naturalistic impersonality presumably represented by Pirandello's early narrative writings.

The assumption of a naturalistic heritage in the Pirandellian novel stems presumably from the reader's feeling of the importance acquired by the narrative material per se. Such an assumption is soon rectified by the counteracting thought that Pirandello's intervention in the core of the novel is felt in the unusual, and to a naturalist writer inconceivable, violence by which his cases explode, submitting the shape of his stories to a tremendous, almost unbearable pressure from within.

From this point of view, Pirandello's initiation as a narrator, which took place well before his essay on humorism was written, is telling. Apparently the plot which brings Marta Ajala of *L'esclusa* to the verge of self-destruction obeys the rules of a naive, overwhelmingly sentimental story. A faithful wife, Marta, married to one Rocco Pentagora is courted by a verbose, middle-aged politician, Gregorio Alvignani; a frustrated epistolographer, he floods her with endless love letters. Marta is compromised by them, becomes a calumniated wife, and then in obedience to the implacably hypocritical rules of a provincial Southern town is expelled from her husband's house and returned to her paternal home. Here her father, deeply wounded by the offense, sacrifices his life on the altar of the infringed laws of honor. He virtually locks himself in his room, never appearing in public again, lets his business go to ruin in the hands of an incompetent and dishonest nephew, and inevitably dies of a stroke. The spell over, the house of Ajala endures. The sister of the unjustly accused Marta cannot find a husband, since offended society prohibits its members from knocking on the door of a family which has betrayed its rules. So Marta is literally compelled to become Alvignani's mistress for good. At this point however, her jealous husband, feeling his solitude and the unjust treatment to which he has submitted his wife, repents and approaches her again with peaceful intentions. The rather corny scene of reconciliation takes place near the bed of Marta's dying mother-in-law— who, by the way, had during her younger years deserted husband and children for a life of adventure, creating a particular sensitivity to waywardness in the vengeful Pentagora family.

The real interest of the story lies beyond the disconcerting plot, in the attention the writer pays to the absurd rules of society and to the reaction of the victimized individual. There is a possible alternative given to human behavior: Francesco Ajala, coherently and uncompromisingly accepting social rules whatever the consequences, chooses the first of the two solutions; his daughter Marta, who rebels against the cruelty of these rules, chooses the second. There is grandeur in Ajala's absurd conformity to the letter of an artificial moral code, as there is courage in Marta's rebellion. But Pirandello's interest does not lie particularly in showing the idiosyncratic aspects of the Ajala family's behavior. Francesco's and Marta's attitudes, so forcefully underlined, appear relevant insofar as they reveal the true laws of life: society cannot afford to forgive a sin which has never been really committed; only when society through its cruel suspicion compels the individual to go astray can a compromise of some sort be reached.

Close in time to the essay on humorism is Pirandello's rather lengthy novel *I vecchi e i giovani* (*The Old and the Young*). This novel is interesting mainly because it touches on the territory explored by "L'umorismo," written the previous year, and is strongly influenced by it. The obstacle to a reading of the novel's plot in a key close to the setting established in the essay is created by the thick wall of historical conventions which the author must dismantle in order to find his way toward the naked truths of life. The operation that becomes quintessential, burning and abrasive in Pirandello's theater, so universal in its typology, loses itself here in a web of episodes all too plausible because they reproduce historical patterns directly witnessed by Pirandello and Pirandello's generation. Benedetto Croce himself, in his *History of Italy from 1871 to 1915*, has spoken of the crisis of a generation which, having been involved in the heroic deeds that brought about the unification of Italy, found itself unable to cope with the daily routine of administering a very composite state, the end result of different economies and diversified cultural traditions. Furthermore, the moral decay of the leading class in Italy had been the object of the fictional inquiry of novelists of the naturalistic school as well, vividly interested in reproducing the experience of the former conspirators—who, having deprived themselves of every pleasure during a youth spent in jail and in exile, turned politicians, then became in their late years involved in the corruption of power. "Corruptio optimi pessima": in *I vecchi e i giovani* the elderly prime minister, Francesco d'Atri, overburdened by his own past as a national hero, betrayed by a wife young enough to be his daughter and by his political allies, who face great financial scandal, confronts the destruction of his political career with a sort of paralysis of the will, an absolute incapability to act.

But if the character of Francesco d'Atri, a cross between two prime ministers who really existed, is on the whole plausibly shaped according to the rules of the naturalistic novel searching for a political *tranche de vie*, then the annihilation of his will to act shows a sharp experimental interference on Pirandello's part that is strictly linked to basic distrust of the objectivity of his characters' motivations. In *I vecchi e i giovani* there are too many people who do not know what they are doing, who even do not do what the circumstances ask them to do. Donna Caterina Auriti and her son Roberto, and even Gerlando Laurentano, the aristocrat who unpredictably takes the side of the Sicilian miners against the government, appear crystallized in their refusal of life in its becoming—prisoners of their past, of "life as form," as the later, philosophical Pirandello would eloquently put it.

Why does all this happen? Why does Pirandello freeze so many characters, extracting them from the stream of the historical narration? In the struggle between the poor *carusi,* relentlessly and hopelessly working in the Sicilian sulphur mines, and the mine-owners, the exploiters, represented in the novel by Flaminio Salvo, Pirandello stands aloof in a position of "humoristic" equidistance. This does not necessarily mean that his sympathy for the revolutionary movement of the Sicilian Fasces is to be categorically denied, against the agreement of his biographers. Rather, it could be said that Pirandello's allegiances appear from the beginning sharply divided. There is on the one hand his moderate heritage according to which any rebellious activity is always an assault against the mystic idea of fatherland, a way of debasing the unity of Italy, so painfully achieved through the sacrifices of a generation. On the other there is his awareness of the social injustices this very unity has brought about.

Were Pirandello only on the side of rebellion, we would not understand why he mobilizes the hero of one of his early poems, Pier Gudrò (a peasant who has fought the wars of the Risorgimento and gives lessons of patriotism to the indifferent and cynical bourgeois), changes his name to Mauro Mortara, and brings him to die at the very end of the novel. Pier Gudrò-Mortara sees in the rebellious miners the enemies of the unified Italy for which he has fought many a battle, therefore he goes against them in fighting trim. Mortara, it is true, happens to be killed by the same Italian troops he is trying to help, and his ultimate fate is to lie dead with the miners he wanted to punish so badly. But all this is brought about by the author, who seems to be interested in confusing the issue on purpose. It is in fact from the ideological chaos involving the events that the humoristic distance of the writer truly stems. In the very heart of the novel a space of reflection is created, a kind of strategic no-man's-land from which the author disembodies and dismantles human emotions, reducing them to their most schematic essence. Pirandello's chosen mouthpiece in the novel, Cosimo Laurentano, dismisses with a tired gesture the story of horror and blood the four young revolutionaries are telling him. "Looking at what happened as if already far away in time," Pirandello explains, "don Cosimo could not see either the sense or the purpose of it. His aspect expressed the same feeling of detachment that emanates from objects which impassibly witness the fleeting passing of human events."

Pirandello's attitude of extracting the characters of his novel from the flux of history shows how profound is his reservation toward any harmony artificially created between thoughts and events, between the world and the human mind. The ever-changing rhythm of life destroys ideals we try to formulize and basically modifies the assumptions on which we build what we pretentiously call our personality. Things do not mean, they are: the meaning we attribute to them is an arbitrary construction, an illusion to be dismantled by the humoristic writer. There are, on the one hand, the subjective illusions and affections which would like to give a direction to the world; on the other there is the world, which stands indifferent and unmodifiable. Nothing is true except the sea, the mountain, the rock, the blade of grass; man cannot be true to himself because he continuously changes, cannot be true to the world because he can neither know nor modify it.

The task of attempting in an ever-renewed act of heroic despair to bridge the gap between the unknown, unpredictable self and the mystery of the universe is entrusted to the character, which Pirandello calls *personaggio*, while the humoristic reestablishment of the implacable truth comes occasionally from a zone of wisdom inhabited by a demiurgic wizard who is Pirandello's mouthpiece. Although this character, observing the plot from the outside, represents a rather archaic tool that will eventually be discarded in the great theatrical works such as *To Clothe the Naked, Henry IV,* and *Six Characters in Search of an Author,* the function of clarification attributed to him in Pirandello's art is not to be underestimated. The role represented in *I vecchi e i giovani* by Cosimo Laurentano is taken over by Serafino Gubbio in *Shoot (Si gira)*—a novel which in 1925, ten years after its first publication in the *Nuova antologia*, appeared under the title *Quaderni di Serafino Gubbio operatore.* Pirandello, who disliked the walking shadows of the talking movies and dreamed of movies made of pure music and pure vision (*cinemelografia*), was in his early years particularly interested in the function of the camera. In the novel *Shoot,* the camera becomes the impassible eye through which all the events are observed; but Gubbio, who operates the camera, becomes the supreme verifier, the one who reads the events, underlining their complexities and their ambiguities. The camera only seizes what happens; the human eye goes deeper into the ambivalence of human actions, detects the ever-changing moods of characters who never are what they were. The heavy burden of this complicated mechanism (camera plus human eye) was eventually simplified in the profoundly modified theatrical version of *Shoot,* entitled *Ciascuno a suo modo (Each in His Own Way).* Here the demiurgic role of Pirandello's mouthpiece shrinks considerably; and although a character, Diego, is called on to interfere dialectically and to extricate his fellow humans from the web of contradictions in which they involve themselves, his reduced role paves the way for a theatrical solution according to which each character agrees to confront the other and erode the other's thesis without intermediaries.

The role of the intermediary still appears decisive in *Così è (se vi pare)*

(*It Is So* [*If You Think So*]), where Laudisi not only leads the story toward its surprising solution, but helps us to discover the laws of hypocrisy and false morality which undermine the "respectable" society of a provincial town, in Italy as elsewhere. The final appearance of Signora Ponza, and her confusing, noncommital statements about her identity, by its humoristic overtones bewilders the spectator in search of a theatrical shock of recognition, defeating his impatience to go home fully reconciled with himself and with the meaning of the story he has been told. Laudisi, though not necessarily identifiable with Pirandello, appears more than anyone else to have grasped the author's awareness that the objective identity of Mrs. Ponza is beyond human reach, a myth of the mind, not a reality.

As far as the artistic destiny of the *personaggio* is concerned, Pirandello goes well beyond the theoretical approach he advocated in "L'umorismo." While in the essay the character's affirmative striving was counteracted and suffocated by an overpowering reflection, in the works of fiction (novels, short stories, theater alike) the character wants the limelight. He tries hard to achieve an *espace vitale* for his suffering, and finally in spite of everything succeeds at least in presenting his case with eloquent despair. In his long-lasting struggle for survival he shouts his truths against the equally vital counterthrusts continuously voiced around him. Henry IV in order to remove the obstacles to his survival artificially avoids any confrontation, finding in the complete isolation of his pretended madness the necessary space for a self-fulfilling statement of his own identity; of course his illusion is destroyed as soon as he is reintegrated into the realm inhabited by his fellow humans. The father and the daughter of *Six Characters in Search of an Author* vehemently defend the truthfulness of their suffering life as characters against the theatrical artifices imposed on them by the Manager. Of course, the truth of each character is challenged and necessarily eroded by the countertruth expressed by his fellow character.

Pirandello's *personaggio* appears to be born under the sign of an everlasting illusion of survival. The more his power of reflection interferes with his illusions, the less willing he is to give them up, the readier to give them another chance. The plots woven around a series of mirages would be very tenuous indeed, were the resistance of the character to annihilation not so incoherently heroic and vital. It could be said that the humoristic technique used by Pirandello, in revealing the truth of the game underneath the illusion, ends by vigorously underlining the pathetic consistency of this very illusion, its power of survival.

The proof of the self-asserting vitality of the illusions can be easily found in the endless drive for narrative experimentation to which Pirandello submits the otherwise one-sided and irreversible statements of his essay on humorism. Let us take, for instance, the assertion that the world—sea, mountains, rocks, blades of grass—exists but does not mean. Pirandello, who knows that human illusion continuously builds bridges to reach the world, to make it meaningful to us, tells the touching story of the love and care displayed by a poor unfrocked deacon, nicknamed Canta l'Epistola, for a blade of grass valiantly resisting the adverse surroundings. When a lady thoughtlessly steps on it, putting an end to its struggle for survival, Canta l'Epistola insults her, provokes her lover, an expert pistoleer, to a duel, and eventually gets killed.

In concluding, we are duly brought to the *vexata quaestio* of the polymorphic aspect of Pirandello's art. Was he an eminent story-teller turned dramatist? Or was his theater on the contrary the late revelation of a genius that long narrative practice had repressed and undermined? If we were to take at face value Pirandello's statement of indifference toward the theater in an unpublished letter to Mario Puccini written as late as 1912, we would be rather puzzled. Was Pirandello's conversion to the theater really by pure chance? A careful reading of his work helps us to state the problem in sounder methodological terms. In analyzing the essay "L'umorismo" in its 1920 edition, we realize that the theoretical approach it advocates is the result of the superimposition of experiences belonging to the large spectrum of Pirandello's literary career. There are statements directly derived from another essay, of 1905, in which the principles of humorism are already formulated; there is also the interpolation of a discussion with Croce which can only follow the first edition of "L'umorismo," reviewed by Croce in 1909. There is even a prelude to the theory of the contrast between life and form that is the belated result of philosopher Adriano Tilgher's bad influence on Pirandello's theater. I could go on, adding other cases such as the incorporation of the episode of *Pier Gudrò,* written in 1894, in the novel *I vecchi e i giovani* of 1909; or the presence of concepts already well known to Pirandello's readers in a lecture on Verga in 1931.

Furthermore, the article "L'azione parlata," which appeared in the Florentine periodical *Marzocco* as early as 1899, greatly anticipates Pirandello's involvement in the theater and a painstakingly Pirandellian theory of the stage. Pirandello confines, for instance, the function of the author to the architecture of the plot; the characters are declared free and independent in expressing their drama. While in D'Annunzio, Pirandello states, all the characters speak the eloquent language of their author and therefore are always D'Annunzio, the author of the new theater ought to be able to multiply himself, complying with the rules of the individualities he is representing. This atomistic theory of the theater, so radically formulated, finds in its extremism the limit and the obstacle to prompt scenic actualization. And it is perhaps in this precocious theoretical radicalism that the reason for Pirandello's belated conversion to the theater lies.

The reading of the essay on humorism, understood as a point of convergence of Pirandello's meditation on art, and the perusal of the article "L'azione parlata," the story "La tragedia d'un personaggio," and the preface to *Six Characters in Search of an Author* help us to realize at once the early formulation of Pirandello's artistic ideology and his aspiration toward a synchronic interchange of all his literary experiences. The youthful discovery of the theory of humorism, and its application for years to a whole extended range of novels and short stories, contains in its seed the decisive advocacy of open theatrical forms that we know is posterior to 1916. But why does Pirandello come to the theater as late as 1916? The moment of theatrical truth is reached when the scheme of the novel appears obsolete in its traditional structures of evasion; when even the rhythm of the short story becomes prejudicial to the basic confrontations of the human instincts the writer is advocating, and another "tempo" is needed for Pirandello's art, in which the spoken word becomes the character's last frontier of self-defense, his only possible action.

RICHARD GILMAN

Pirandello

Among the late entries in the journal or notebook which Luigi Pirandello kept during most of his life as a writer one finds this remark: "There is somebody who is living my life and I know nothing about him." The assumption of an unknown self, an *other* who fills the same space as one's own and breathes the same air, is by no means unheard of among writers, but in Pirandello it becomes central, obsessive, and, seized as a painful inspiration, one of the very principles of imaginative procedure. Pirandello is one of the great dramatic technicians of alienation, one of the foremost theatrical poets of self-division and internal abyss. He is also, as a function of the foregoing, the great modern playwright of the theater, or the theatrical, as *subject;* in his work the full, radical questioning of the stage as a place of formal pretending begins. To have instigated this is to have brought what we loosely call "modern" drama into a phase whose end is not yet in sight.

Pirandello's drama may be said to move between the key words "mirror" and "mask," both of which, in addition to being nouns of doubleness, implying something—a face, a self?—standing outside or beneath, are eminently theatrical metaphors. His dramatic work has been spoken of as constituting *il teatro dello specchio,* the theater of the mirror, and the word or object occurs over and over again in his writing. Furthermore, he gave to every volume of his collected plays the same title, *Naked Masks,* the implication of which is vulnerability in deception, the impossibility of being truly disguised.

Pirandellian drama comes into being at a point when that revolution

From *The Making of Modern Drama.* © 1972, 1973, 1974 by Richard Gilman. Farrar, Straus & Giroux, 1974.

in Western thought and art which we call Modernism is in full tide, having passed from unsettling discovery and invention to acceptance or at least legitimacy. Influenced himself by Nietzsche, Bergson, and—doubtless at first unconsciously, by cultural osmosis—Freud, Pirandello quickly takes his place among the masters of the displacement of values and the reorganization of consciousness. There is a story that after a performance in Germany by Pirandello's theater group Albert Einstein went up to him and told him that "we are kindred souls." The incident may be apocryphal, but in that case its having been invented testifies to Pirandello's position and stature.

It testifies more particularly to the generally held belief that Pirandello's central and peculiarly contemporary quality as a writer is his "relativism," and that his major achievement lies in having infused the drama, that obdurately absolutist medium, with a principle of uncertainty and doubt. There is truth in this, but elevated into a full-scale interpretation it has resulted in a kind of debased Pirandellianism. Here the description is of a mildly Satanic figure—neat, pointy Vandyke, eyes narrowed in an ironic, worldly glance—who presides over a theater of mockery and deflation, an exhibition hall for the overturning of intellectual pieties and the destruction of conventional, optimistic wisdom.

There is a coarser but somewhat related portrait of Pirandello as the dramatist par excellence of "illusion and reality," as if their relationship had not been either the outright subject or unstated ground of great segments of drama before him. Pirandello indeed sometimes seems to encourage this view of his art: "Why is he always harping on this illusion and reality business?" a character in one of his own plays asks. But it is a strategic move on the playwright's part; he knows what is being said about him and, most to his purposes, that the talk issues from the very misunderstanding of the nature of human existence his drama is partly designed to expose. Things are not either illusion or reality, but both, and to make this truth present on the stage is one driving purpose of Pirandello's complex dramatic art.

The complexity is great enough to account for the persistent popular and academic attempt to reduce it, to bring it into that system of abstract valuation and narrow identification by which we make cultural history manageable. It is easier for us to think of Shaw as "wit," and Chekhov as "mood," Ibsen as "social problem," Strindberg as "sexual struggle," and so on, than to try to discover the ways in which their respective arts transcend what may seem to be their own leading thesis or coloration. In the case of Pirandello, the "harping" on illusion and reality, on masks, mirrors, doubleness, estrangement, etc., has resulted in a widespread conviction that for better or worse (although mostly worse) he is an "intellectual" playwright, cerebral, moved by ideas rather than emotions, a dramatist who has forsworn the traditional passions of the stage in order to employ it for the exhibition of a species of exacerbated thought.

Once again, the mistake is to think in mutually exclusive alternatives: the heart or the head, passion or intellect. It's a commonplace to say that the source of an error like this is in our general need for dichotomy, our Manichaean division of ourselves and the world into competing systems or powers. But there is a specifically aesthetic origin—or rather one rooted in the sociology and psychology of traditional response to theater—of the notion that Pirandello is cerebral at the expense of emotion. And this is our assumption that the very purpose of the stage is to be an arena for the display of passions in conflict, that because of its physicality, its *fleshiness* and principle of palpable encounter, the theater gives us our own selves represented as embodied emotions.

What the theater of course gives us, or ought to give us, is consciousness; consciousness *enacted,* so to speak. Moreover, in this enterprise, emotion, or passion, figures as an element placed or located in relation to other things. The theater of the Greeks or Elizabethans or of the seventeenth century is one in which such situating of emotion is paramount, and it is the very mark of the decline of the stage in the eighteenth and nineteenth centuries that this action is relinquished and the direct presentation of emotion for its own sake becomes dominant. What we really mean by melodrama is theater in which emotion is offered without consciousness—which might be described as the *understanding of emotion.* In this case, action, which in Aristotle's sense meant the physical unfolding of morally and spiritually fraught events, is, as Henry James observed, converted into mere "sensation."

The modern theater, beginning with the isolated and only much later to be discovered plays of Büchner in the 1830s, can be said to comprise an effort to return the stage to its original function of the enactment of consciousness. In this light, innovation can be seen to involve strategies of the formal conquest of "bad habits," the restoration of health and efficacy to a corrupted or denatured organism. This is what Ionesco meant when he remarked that the avant-garde always seeks to return to some earlier condition, that it is not antihistorical but simply opposed to its own immediately preceding history, the time of an art's deflection or impoverishment.

As one of the dramatic imaginations who rescued the stage from its own long illness, Pirandello's innovative energy naturally took its own special form. In the roughest of classifications we can say that Ibsen infused social experience with moral awareness, Strindberg released unconscious truths, Chekhov set forth the action of time in human existence. Pirandello's accomplishment was to overcome the gap which had been present between intellect and passion, and he did this not, as his detractors say, by elaborating a cerebral drama but by breaking down the reigning distinction. He himself wrote that "one of the novelties [a word that might better be translated from the Italian as 'newnesses,' 'new things'] that I have given to modern drama consists in converting the intellect into passion."

He might with almost as much justice have said that he had also given to passion a forgotten intellectual dimension or mode. The point is that in Pirandello's work consciousness plays back and forth between feeling and idea and is the very result of their relations, their reciprocity and tension. We know what we feel and feel what we know, he is saying, or rather, we can *think* our feelings and feel our thoughts. The source of the criticism of Pirandello for being overintellectual lies in a wish to keep the categories separate, to keep intellect from introducing a principle of abstraction into the pulsing body of direct and hard-breathing representation of feelings we consider serious theater to be.

This desire to keep uncontaminated the theater conceived of as a place for feeling and not thought is persistent and perhaps ineradicable. In 1970 the young Austrian playwright Peter Handke, whose highly "intellectual" drama has disconcerted audiences and critics alike, was asked by an interviewer whether his work wasn't too cerebral at the expense of emotion. "I can't separate the rational and emotional effects," he replied, and they are indeed inseparable in his work. "Doesn't a stunning new thought, a new insight, a new view that is based on reason, often make you feel wholly emotional effects?" he went on. As different as Pirandello's theater is from Handke's, they are both within the century-long line of questioning of received wisdom about the place of thought on the stage.

During the 1880s August Strindberg gave up writing plays for a period of three or four years because he considered the stage to be "reprehensible." It was, he said, "mere pose, superficiality and calculation"; compared to fiction or poetry, it had no place for technical originality and, most crucially, for thought. Before this suspension of his dramatic work Strindberg had written a number of lengthy plays, mostly on historical themes and almost all of an unexceptionably traditional kind. When he returned to the theater he had found a principle out of which to elaborate a new dramatic consciousness, first expressed in the savage beauties and revelatory dissonances of *The Father* and *Miss Julie*.

Pirandello was never as explicit about his misgivings concerning the theater as a place for new consciousness as Strindberg had been (or Chekhov, who "swore fearfully" at the "conventions of the stage"). But the evidence is that for a long time after he had begun his career as an imaginative writer Pirandello thought of the theater as a very much lesser form than fiction and only turned seriously to it when, like Strindberg, he had succeeded in fashioning for himself a radically new approach to the nature of dramatic art and had gained the morale—the confidence, even arrogance—necessary to defy prevailing expectations and definitions.

Luigi Pirandello comes out of a Sicilian rather than an Italian literary tradition and, as shadowy as such regional distinctions may be, out of a Sicilian rather than an Italian psychic and imaginative ground. One biographical fact that may be significant is that he came from an upper-class and presumably sophisticated family, unlike his great Sicilian literary predecessor and influence, Giovanni Verga. His father, a wealthy owner of sulphur mines, could afford to send him to study abroad, and Luigi, who had indicated literary talent by writing poetry at an early age, went at eighteen in 1885 to the University of Rome and later to Bonn, where he was greatly influenced by that institution's notable school of philology.

Another pertinent biographical fact, though one of which perhaps too much has been made in an attempt to explain his "gloom" and dark humor, was his deeply oppressive marriage. This was an arranged affair; the bride was the daughter of a business associate of his father and Pirandello had scarcely seen her before the wedding day. A few years later she began to show signs of mental disturbance, which rapidly developed into full-scale psychosis. Her chief symptom was a paranoid suspicion that Pirandello was betraying her, even with their own daughter, and to appease her he refrained from going out at night for many years. Urged to have her committed, he declared it his duty to stay by her, and it was not until 1918, with the illness growing more severe, that he at last placed her in a mental institution, where she soon after died. Later Pirandello was to say that "a madwoman had led his hand for fifteen long years."

Before fame as a playwright came to him in the 1920s Pirandello had achieved a solid if not spectacular reputation for his short stories and novels and for a handful of influential essays on literary-philosophical themes. His earliest stories, written during the 1890s, were thoroughly Sicilian in milieu and tone, full of local color and, although largely "naturalistic" in style, characterized by a rather non-naturalistic interest in extreme and even bizarre passions and by an almost mythical sense of fatality. Later he transferred his fictional scene to Italy; his stories became more "modern," urban, psychological, and, as we would now describe them, existential.

He was to continue to write stories even after the stage had become his major activity (he once said that he wanted to write one for every day in the year, and ended about a hundred short) and, against the popular wisdom which holds that the two enterprises ought to remain wholly separate and distinct, maintained an unusually close relationship between his fiction and his theater work. The majority of his thirteen one-act plays and several of his full-length ones were directly derived from his short stories, and the seeds of a number of others are to be found in the fiction. This in fact has contributed to the criticism that his plays were mostly "dramatized" fiction, that he was not a "true" playwright because he thought narratively or novelistically and not in histrionic ways.

This judgment stems from the kind of rigidity in thinking about drama that was described earlier. To the academic or categorical mind, drama and fiction—like all the arts—ought to obey entirely different principles, so that the muddying of such distinctions, which is in fact one of the consciously engendered marks of modern sensibility, has been a source of disgust and even scandal. As we have seen, Pirandello himself felt a conflict between the two modes of expression, becoming able to reconcile them only after he had freed himself from his own submission to conventional notions of what drama ought to be and do.

In any case, it is possible to see in Pirandello's earlier fiction a number of ideas, themes, and imaginative dispositions that would naturally gravitate toward theatrical expression (not "dramatization") once techniques for their histrionic incarnation had been achieved. His first novel, *The Late Mattia Pascal* (1904), is a case in point. This startlingly "advanced" tale of a man who, when an accident victim is mistaken for him and buried under his name, is given the chance to create a new identity, is suffused in that atmosphere of agitated metaphysical concern and painful consciousness of the self's ambiguities which will characterize the great plays. In the same way, a later novel, *Shoot* (1916), the story of a movie cameraman who desperately wishes to get at the truth, the "real" lives of the performers whose fictive existences he records, is deeply involved with what will be one of Pirandello's central dramatic ideas.

For a long time Pirandello's writing for the theater was occasional and subordinate; his first play, *The Vise,* was written in 1898, but not produced until 1910, and there is no record of his having written another dramatic work in the interval. From then on, until his sudden emergence as a leading playwright toward the end of World War I, he wrote a handful of one-act plays and two or three full-length ones, whose generally minor status in his own mind is indicated by their having mostly been written in Sicilian dialect, something he had long since given up in his fiction. Later some of these plays were to be translated into Italian by Pirandello himself and others. But almost nothing in this early dramatic work indicates more than a conventional talent, although one might consider that its idiosyncratic violence and increasing psychological emphasis might be portents of something larger to come.

He had not yet found a way to make the stage serve the ideas which agitated and tormented him, ideas—perspectives on human dilemmas, really—that had already found their way into his fiction. These perspectives are to be found in their clearest and most direct form in an essay he wrote in 1908 called "On Humor." A humorist, which was what he considered himself to be, was, he argued, a person who worked, consciously or not, in the space between the convictions mankind has about itself and the world and the truth, which, whatever it might be, is not to be discovered in those convictions. "One of the greatest humorists, without knowing it," Pirandello wrote, "was Copernicus, who took apart not the machine of the universe, but the proud image which we had made of it."

The essay contains statements of what are to become the leading intellectual motifs of his great plays and reveals his large debt to Bergson, among others. "What we know about ourselves is but a part, perhaps a very small part of what we are," he wrote, and again: "To man is given at birth the sad privilege of feeling himself alive, with the illusions which come from it—namely to assume a reality outside himself and that interior feeling of life, changeable and various." Perhaps most Bergsonian of all is the following sentence: "The forms in which we try to stop and fix the continuous flow are the concepts, the ideals within which we want to keep coherent all the fictions we create, the condition and status in which we try to establish ourselves."

As a humorist his task was to try to deal with the discrepancy between the forms of the mind and the flow of life, between fiction and reality. Some years later he was to compose in the introduction to *Six Characters in Search of an Author* a coolly appraising intellectual self-portrait which went even further than had the essay on humor toward defining his particular literary character and temperament:

> To me it was never enough to present a man or a woman and what is special and characteristic about them simply for the pleasure of presenting them; to narrate a particular affair, lively or sad, simply for the pleasure of narrating it; to describe a landscape simply for the pleasure of describing it. There are some writers (and not a few) who do feel this pleasure and, satisfied, ask no more. They are, to speak more precisely, historical writers.

But there are others who, beyond such pleasure, feel a more profound spiritual need on whose account they admit only figures, affairs, landscapes which have been soaked, so to speak, in a particular sense of life and acquire from it a universal value. These are, more precisely, philosophical writers. I have the misfortune to belong to these last.

The "misfortune" he speaks of has of course to do with the additional burden of consciousness such philosophical writers (and they include all the makers of modern drama) have had to bear; instead of being the re-creation of the world and of experience through a language and an imaginative mode ready at hand, the task of a writer like Pirandello is to find the language, the literary means, for a new creation. The position of the innovator is therefore that of one who has to invent, bring into being, what his temperament and sense of life find absent from the inherited artistic means at his disposal, and this has to be accomplished in the face of the innate conservatism, the entropic tendency, of already accomplished consciousness.

ANNE PAOLUCCI

Comedy and Paradox in Pirandello's Plays (An Hegelian Perspective)

The temptation will always be strong, for those of us analyzing any aspect of Pirandellian comedy, to begin with an examination—or at least a brief assessment—of the playwright's well-known little book "L'umorismo" ("On Humor"). I have not wholly resisted that temptation, but I have tried to on two grounds. First, Pirandello's exposition in that book has been carefully examined and evaluated by such experts as Professor Dante della Terza, whose incisive essay "On Pirandello's Humorism" has proved invaluable to most of us interested in the subject, and Professor Antonio Illiano, whose translation of "L'umorismo" (with Daniel Testa) supplies indispensable notes as well as a fine introduction.

My second reason for resisting the temptation of using "L'umorismo" as my own critical base in this paper is, I suppose, my own *sentimento del contrario*. That feeling—as Professor della Terza interprets Pirandello's use of the term—is a sort of categorical imperative. It indicates, della Terza very acutely observes, "the presence of a subjective 'feeling' that somewhere in the stratified world of our affections there is an emotional explosion that shakes our privileged heritage of sentiments, refusing to accept them as the only ones which really 'are.' "

I experience that sort of explosion when I read "L'umorismo," or Croce's criticism of it, or the debate over Tilgher's influence on Pirandello, or Pirandello's responses. Pirandello the literary critic and aesthetician becomes for me, then, simply another character in another Pirandellian play. The experience makes it impossible for me to read Pirandello's discussion of humor

From *Modern Drama* 20, no. 4 (December 1977). © 1977 by the University of Toronto, Graduate Centre for Study of Drama.

as if I thought he were trying simply to be a critical philosopher. What is revealed there is the genius of the comic playwright. The plays have yet to be written; but when they are finally written, it is humor, the *feeling* of the opposite, as distinguished from mere *perception* of the opposite, that will constantly be applied in the best of them. The object of its application is not to form some substantive thing before us that we can then view at leisure, but rather to dissolve what we have before us and show that there is really nothing there—except the imaginative will of the artist functioning as an irresistible dissolvent.

"Pirandello's definition of humorism" (della Terza writes) "indicates a dilemma at the core of his aesthetic convictions." His "feeling" of the opposite is not a feeling, not a sentiment at all, "since its activity is overwhelmingly critical, analytical, and rational. By trying to give another name to a cognitive activity Pirandello, instead of making his dilemma inconspicuous, as he would have liked, ends up by giving the limelight, unwittingly but revealingly, to an all-encompassing and proliferating imagery suggested by the intrusive concept of reflection."

Read as a revelation of Pirandello's developing dramatic attitude, the essay is surely invaluable. But we simply must not mistake it for an empirically based theory of his own dramaturgical achievement. In that respect I think his essay on the history of the Italian theater is much more illuminating; and I shall have occasion to cite it later. The essay on humor, with its sharp distinction of the comic from the humorous, makes it difficult moreover to relate its meaning to the main content of aesthetic theory which, at least as it relates to drama, does not insist on such a distinction. Comedy, from Aristophanes to Shakespeare and beyond, down to Pirandello himself, of course, has been the chief medium of expression for humor in Pirandello's sense. Neither etymology nor usage justifies insistence on a distinction that assigns the use of "comic" to mere "perception of the opposite." Where I have tried, in what follows, to relate my discussion to the main current of aesthetic theory, I have turned for clarification more often than not to Hegel's usage, which, insofar as it is supported by an organically integrative system of thought, avoids the pitfalls of mere trial and error.

I was struck recently by the closing paragraph of a book on *Humor in Pascal,* that most paradoxical of all modern thinkers. Summarizing the "density of techniques" of what she pointedly calls the "comic humor" of Pascal (to distinguish it from other kinds of humor and other uses of the comic), the author, Professor Olga Russell, supplies us with a long list of distinctions that may be drawn in analyzing the effects of a paradoxical approach to what were for Pascal—as for Pirandello—the "shows of life."

The main techniques of comic humor bring to focus, the author writes, "the unexpected within a sentence, or in a situation, or in a figure of speech; the grotesque, the incongruous; caricature by gesture; belittling humor, irony in an adjective, or an adverb, or a verb (in the midst of an otherwise straightforward, serious sentence); irony through disproportion, or by metaphor within metaphor; dynamic and comic antithesis of the small cause and the vast result; the use of derogatory terms or names bringing characters to life in conversation; juxtaposition of the concrete and the abstract, forcing the reader to smile in the obvious attitude of common sense; onomatopoeia as effective as gesture seen on the stage; imagery, concrete and vivid, to point up unreasonableness and foolishness; true comic situations and characters, as in charlatanry in medicine; dramatic situation and crescendo in effect to light up the ridiculous (so close to the sublime); traditional comic themes, *le dupeur dupé,* raised to symbolic meaning; costume as symbol; and the tones of light raillery, teasing, gentle irony, sarcasm, bitter and violent satire." The author adds that the "humorous effects" of these techniques are "effective for being presented courteously and charitably, in that Pascal shares with all men the burden of human foolishness."

Pirandello makes the same point in "L'umorismo," citing De Sanctis's estimate of Machiavelli's "tolerance that understands and absolves," and stressing how the author of *Don Quixote* makes it difficult for us actually to laugh at his hero by troubling us with feelings not only of pity, but "even, indeed, of admiration." Yet I think it is fair to say that Pirandello applies his comic art with an exhaustive thoroughness (at least in his best plays) that is not to be found in a Pascal or a Cervantes. In the closing pages of "L'umorismo," it is the destructive or decompositional thoroughness of his *sentimento del contrario* that is emphasized. Where the ordinary artist, the ordinary epic or dramatic poet, will *compose* a character from opposite and contrasting elements, the true humorist will do "just the opposite: he will *decompose* the character into his elements." The true humorist applies a conditional "if," which is but a minute particle of doubt, to begin with—but it is a "minute particle which can be pinned to, and inserted like a wedge into, all events." Inserting that wedge, hammering it into the seemingly solid substance of his subject everywhere, the true humorist literally decomposes what ordinary art composes: "hence," in Pirandello's words, "all that is disorganized, unraveled and whimsical, all the digressions which can be seen in the works of humor, as opposed to the ordered construction, the *composition* of the works of art in general."

That surely is the effect of Pirandello's *sentimento del contrario* in his best plays: it penetrates the subject everywhere, cracks its solidity, till decomposition is inevitable. Situations, events, characters, thoughts—all are overwhelmed, pinned with conditionals, hammered till they are shattered, at least in our reflection, into myriad mirrored fragments. If we attempt to piece the fragments together like a jigsaw puzzle, what we get is not a cracked impression of the original thing, but the personality of the comic artist who has made it all his very own precisely in order to dissolve its apparent rigidity.

In my own view, Pirandello's sense of humor could not have had full scope till he turned artistically from narrative expression (which must be objective in what it attempts to tell of human experience) to dramatic expression (which absorbs the objective in the subjective and vice versa). To *feel* the opposite, rather than perceive it merely, is a labor of the dramatic imagination. We all engagte in it in some measure day in and day out; but it is the dramatist who brings such labor to full artistic birth in the form of tragedy or comedy, or a mixture of the two. But all the world's a stage! the dramatic imagination cries. And it is when he is convinced that the world is indeed but a place leveled out for players upon which to strut and fret their hour that a dramatic intelligence can begin to people it with such players. The necessity of dramatic art, its reason for being, is to be sought in that perception; it helps us to obey the Delphic Oracle's command to "know thyself." A stage must be cleared so that we can come to see ourselves as we are, in rational reflection. We *are* what reflective reasoning shows us to be. Yet, when that viewing has been done in any society, a time inevitably follows when the reflection hardens so as to become impenetrable; and then, isntead of being itself perceived as a rational reflection, rationally real in itself, it becomes for us merely a reflecting surface in which we imagine we see our subjective selves reflected as opposite. The comic spirit, according to Hegel, shatters that hardness, dissolves it, so that comedy is always a reaction to some other form of drama, whether ceremonial in the religious sense, or tragic.

Pirandello, as I said, coming late to the task, does this sort of comic work with a thoroughness that is positively exhaustive. But what exactly is it that he views thus humorously in an exhaustive way? It is absurd to say— bearing in mind that we are talking about a man who invaded the early twentieth-century European stage like a conqueror with his *Six Characters in Search of an Author*—that it is life in general. Pirandello had already applied his *sentimento del contrario* to life in general. What is life in general? As many things as there are minds, and instants of experience in each mind to perceive its endless flow of multiplicity. *Uno, nessuno, o centomila, Così è (se vi pare)*—we are the flitting shadows of a dream, with no idea who or what it is that casts such ever-changing shadows.

By the time Pirandello has begun to put his own plays on stage, he has long since swept away mere life as an object of artistic, critical, analytical, overwhelming reflection. He has perceived the opposite in life, and perceived the opposite of that opposite myriadfold. And it is out of the depths of mirrored opposites that he brings up his dramatis personae as creatures of his *sentimento del contrario,* the feeling of the opposite.

Who is Uncle Simone in *Liolà*? Who is Enrico IV? Who is Signora Ponza? *Liolà* is early, so let us begin with Uncle Simone. He claims to be a sexually potent old man who could have a child by his young wife, Mita, if she were fertile, and he has sought to prove his potency to the world by allowing wicked Tuzza and her mother, Zia Croce, to claim that he has fathered the child with whom Tuzza is pregnant. We can see through Uncle Simone's pretense; we can see easily the opposite. And the effect is most comical when Uncle Simone attempts to suggest that he might still father a child with his own wife. Zia Croce heightens the comic effect: it is *no* at seventy; will it be *yes* at eighty-five? It could be, says Uncle Simone. We must leave time `. . . for time. But we—who read and see the play—know already at this point what Zia Croce and Tuzza do *not* know: that Uncle Simone is comical for them at the same moment that he becomes humorous—in Pirandello's sense of the terms—for *us.* It is true that he cannot father a child with Mita; but he can, in fact, father one with her in the same way that he allegedly fathered one with Tuzza. "It's Liolà! I knew it!" Mother and daughter recognize a real opposite to what they thought they had seen—laughable to them and to us, at first; but now they can only gnash their teeth in frustration. *We* smile. It is not perception of the opposite; it is *feeling* of the opposite, *sentimento del contrario.* Uncle Simone is what he is: an impotent old man who wants an heir. His first wife, who died without bearing him a child, asked him on her deathbed to get himself a son. God knows he tried. He seemed to be a fool in trying. In self-defense, his wife cuckolds him. A complex sort of fool. In claiming Tuzza's child, he had announced, in a sense, his willingness to be thus cuckolded. If only God's grace would fill Mita as it had filled Mary! But Simone wants a child of his own, not another Christ. If only his young wife could be filled . . . as Tuzza was filled . . . so that I can have a child by her as I have been ready to claim I had one from Tuzza!

There is something clearly exhaustive in the sense indicated earlier about such humor; certainly it is present in *Six Characters.* The actors who play the characters are not supposed to be actors. They are characters that actors are supposed to play but cannot. They emphasize the difference between what *they* are and what those so-called actors who are trying to play them are. We have paired perceptions of opposites here, as in the case of Uncle Simone. When the curtain comes down, we applaud the actors who have acted the parts of characters that are too real to be played. We recall, perhaps, Hamlet's speech on the subject, marveling that this mere player could act a part so realistically, so passionately, while I—Hamlet—who am *very I,* cannot match the actor's expression of passion. Pirandello's six characters must play a whole play in the mood of that Hamlet speech. It is a daring tour de force, but a tour de force still, as compared with *Hamlet* and as compared with Pirandello's own version of *Hamlet, Enrico IV.*

There is a powerful suggestion of the opposite generated in *Enrico IV,* and there is also a powerful compounded *feeling* of the opposite. There is much to make one smile in Pirandello's masterpiece—but we could hardly call it humor. Or rather, if there is humor, again let me say, the effect is exhaustive. Pirandello's *feeling of the opposite* presses the humorous to its absolute limits and beyond.

I must admit I have been pressing an Hegelian insight here. Hegel says that it is dramatic comedy and humor in the broadest sense that exhaust all of art. In his lectures on *Aesthetics,* he has a brief subsection called "The Comic Treatment of Contingency" ("Die komische Behandlung der Zufälligkeit") and another titled "Subjective Humor" ("Der subjektive Humor") in which he argues that art's dissolution comes finally not with a tragic bang or a melodramatic whimper but with a comic too-sad-to-laugh smile—or what Pirandello calls humor.

"In humor," Hegel says, "it is the person of the artist which comes on the scene in both its superficial and deeper aspects, so that what is at issue there is essentially the spiritual worth of his personality." Humor, as we noted already, has as its object not to develop and shape a thing before us, but to dissolve what is already ours. In Hegel's words again: "It is the artist himself who enters the material, with the result that his chief activity, by the power of subjective notions, flashes of thought, striking modes of interpretation, consists in destroying and dissolving everything that proposes to make itself objective and win a firm shape for itself in reality, or that seems to have such a shape already in the external world."

According to Hegel, art is most taxed when it is made to sustain a humorous attitude (the *sentimento del contrario* interpreted in a genuinely Hegelian sense) toward its subject matter. At the very end of his long lectures on aesthetics, after he has reviewed the entire progression of the arts from architecture through poetry, from the symbolic and classical through the romantic, Hegel speaks finally of dramatic comedy in terms that make me think as much of Pirandello's major figures as of Shakespeare's great Falstaff. A *perception* of the opposite intensified as *feeling* of the opposite is involved in tragedy, as Hegel understands it, as well as in comedy. The "clash of opposites" in tragedy results either in the destruction of the characters who sustain the opposition through one-sided willfulness or in a profound internal conversion that involves acceptance of what had been most seriously resisted. "In comedy," on the other hand, says Hegel, "there comes before our contemplation, in the laughter in which the characters dissolve everything, including themselves, the victory of their own subjective personality which nevertheless persists self-assured." Distinguishing the comical from the laughable, however, Hegel adds: "The comical as such implies an infinite light-heartedness and confidence felt by someone raised altogether above his own inner contradiction and not bitter or miserable in it at all: this is the bliss and ease of a man who, being sure of himself, can bear the frustration of his aims and achievements." And he goes on: ". . . truly *tragic* action necessarily presupposes either a live conception of *individual* freedom and independence or at least an individual's determination and willingness to accept freely and on his own account the responsibility for his own act and its consequences; and for the emergence of *comedy* there must have asserted itself in a still higher degree the free right of the subjective personality and its self-assured dominion."

A. C. Bradley—the great Shakespearean critic—saw, with Hegel's help, the indissoluble link between the comic Falstaff, who drinks and cavorts with Prince Hal, and the final Falstaff, who is rejected by King Henry V. Falstaff's humor is sustained by depth of feeling. "True humor," Hegel writes, "requires great depth and wealth of spirit in order to raise the purely subjective appearance into what is actually expressive, and to make what is substantial emerge out of contingency, out of mere notions." If he is a genuine humorist, the author must proceed with ease, with effortless, unostentatious lightness of expression which, paradoxically, in its very "triviality affords precisely the supreme idea of depth; and since here there are just individual details which gush forth without any order, their inner connection must lie all the deeper and send forth the ray of spirit in their disconnectedness as such."

In his last plays, Pirandello gives us some very deliberate indications of the depths that sustain the paradoxical multiplicity of his art. But the magic of the god-wizard Cotrone (Pirandello's Prospero) in the first play of his great mythic trilogy—*The Mountain Giants (I giganti della montagna)*—is already present in *Liolà*. Cotrone's house is a place where creatures of the imagination are given, in the mere act of imagining them, a local habitation and a name. The world of *Liolà* is perhaps the greatest proof that Pirandello really had such magic power and did not merely talk about it. Illuminating in this respect is what Hegel has to say of the *level* of humor on which Pirandello, in our view, attempts to operate in *Liolà*. In civilized societies of which we have record, art that draws its materials and especially its characters from the lower classes, Hegel says, tends almost invariably to be comic, for it cannot make the deeds of people externally restricted (as the lower classes are on all sides) seriously tragic. The lower-class character can "put on airs" of importance, but he cannot *be* important. If he persists in putting on such airs, he becomes comical. Comic characters have the right to spread themselves in whatever way they wish and can do so claiming an independence of action which— because of their restricted potential—is immediately annihilated by themselves, by what they *are*, and by their inner and outer dependence. "But, above all," says Hegel, "this assumed self-reliance founders on external conditions and the distorted attitude of individuals to them. The power of these conditions is on a totally different level for the lower classes from what it is for rulers and princes."

Hegel is not saying that the comic is limited to the lower classes; he is merely pointing out that lower-class characters have a potentially comic effectiveness. A lower-class type with money, for example, who imagines that his money will take him out of the lower class culturally—someone, say, like Nicia in *Mandragola*—is an example of this kind of comic type. Molière's M. Jourdain is another. And so on.

For Hegel, comedy assumes high dramatic importance—side by side with tragedy—as the vehicle for "pathos," which he defines as the "proper center, the true domain of art." In discussing what he calls the "dissolution of the classical form of art," he observes that comedy cannot rest content with perception of a mere opposition between abiding spiritual values and external contingency. Perception of that kind of opposition, says Hegel in a very Pirandellian mood, is merely prosaic. It takes us, in fact, *out* of the world of art. Comedy must, if not resolve, at least *dis*solve that opposition artistically. True comedy does this by reversing roles, by showing the sham of good intentions and the positive value of a much condemned social order. "Of this kind of art," he writes, "an example is comedy as Aristophanes among the Greeks has handled it without anger, in pure and serene . . . relation to the most essential spheres in the world of his time."

Hegel extends his observations on the comic and the lower classes into his discussion of painting. I shall not go into his argument except to note what may interest us here in a special way. Using examples from German and Dutch painting, where the subject matter is often taken from the crudest and most vulgar levels of society, Hegel notes that such painting offers us scenes "so completely penetrated by . . . cheerfulness . . . that the real subject matter is not vulgarity, which is just vulgar and vicious, but this cheerfulness . . . roguish and comic . . . the Sunday of Life which equalizes everything and removes all evil." The comic aspect, he explains, cancels what is bad and vulgar, and leaves a very *positive* feeling. What better example *of sentimento del contrario?* And what better illustration than Pirandello's Liolà—that amoral rogue (the windmill song is the best testimony of this side of his character)—who, in response to Uncle Simone's charge that he, Liolà, is after the old man's money, can sing a love song which is, in Hegel's terms, "the Sunday of life which equalizes everything and removes all evil"? When Eric Bentley writes that we must enter Pirandello's world through *Liolà*, he reminds us of the difference between the genuine Pirandello and modern Pirandellianism, which is pseudo-Pirandellian precisely because it does not have beneath it, around and above it, the Sicilian "Sunday" comedy of *Liolà*. Comedy, in the sense in which Hegel here describes it, is the *redemption* of the vulgar and the bad, just as the substantive drama of Samuel Beckett and Edward Albee, for example, is the *redemption* of the absurd.

Illuminating, with respect to Pirandello's art, is Hegel's reminder that, in assessing comic power, one needs to be careful to "distinguish whether the dramatis personae are comical in themselves or only in the eyes of the audience." Only the former case, he says—agreeing with Aristotle—can be considered comical in the strict sense, as distinguished from the merely laughable. Plautus and Terence preferred the opposite, and their attitude has, of course, dominated modern theatrical entertainment. Pirandello holds with the Aristotelian view, of course, and it lies at the base of his distinction between the merely comical and the humorous in his early essay. Yet surely he is not, any more than Hegel, beneath appreciating the marvelous combination of the two in Falstaff, for instance. We all have at least a vague recollection of Falstaff's famous self-estimate: but most of us, I venture to say, find ourselves enriched (I know I have!) when we turn to Shakespeare's *ipsissima verba*—as I have in this case. Falstaff says: "The brain of this foolish-compounded clay, man, is not able to invent anything that intends to laughter, more than I invent or is invented on me. I am not only witty in myself, but the cause that wit is in other men." On the subject of Shakespeare's treatment of vulgar characters generally, Hegel points out that in the mature comedies they are aggrandized and enhanced above themselves: "Stephano, Trinculo, Pistol, and the absolute hero of them all, Falstaff, remain sunk in their vulgarity, but at the same time they are shown to be men of intelligence with a genius fit for anything, enabling them to have an entirely free existence, and, in short, to be what great men are. . . . In Shakespeare we find no justification, no condemnation, but only an observation of . . . universal fate; . . . and from that standpoint they see everything perish, themselves included, as if they saw it all happening outside themselves."

Pirandello does not touch much on the comic genius of Shakespeare in "L'umorismo," where, in fact, he cites with approval Giorgio Arcoleo's view that Hamlet is an instance of the first phase of humor which consists in being able to *"laugh at one's own thought."* But it is plain that he appreciates the kind of humor that Hegel has in mind in praising Shakespeare's characterization of Falstaff. In his essay on the history of the Italian Theater, Pirandello dwells especially on the side of that history where its vitality is traced back to the "life of the Theatre" itself, which is to say, the experience of the *commedia dell'arte.* We see there, he writes, "actors . . . who begin by writing the comedies they later perform, comedies at once more theatrical because not written in the isolated study," but in the theater itself. "The transitory, impassioned life of the Theater," he goes on to say, "must have taken such full possession of them that the only interest left to them was that of the spectacle itself—a complete absorption in the quality of the performance and communication with the audience. They are no longer authors; but they are no longer even actors, in the true sense of the word." That, according to Pirandello, was the indispensable experience of living theater that permitted Italy, and Italy alone, to dissolve the rigidity of Renaissance forms so that it could "boast of having drained the recovered classical world of all that it had to offer."

What the *commedia dell'arte* did to shatter the rigidity of the Renaissance inheritance, Pirandello understood himself to be doing, dramatically, with the rigidities of a modern theater that had lost contact with its living origins. For an antecedent, he points to Goldoni. Goldoni had learned the lesson of the *commedia dell'arte* even as Molière and Shakespeare had already learned it. But Goldoni had also done something else of even greater importance, from Pirandello's perspective:

> We will never discover the true Goldoni if we fix our attention on the characters that, according to the fashion of the time, he too tried to create—the good-natured boor, the grumbler, the miser, etc. They are indeed marvelous; but in the comedies in which they appear as protagonists the truly great author reveals himself, on the contrary, in the subordinate characters, one of whom—the little housemaid, for example—suddenly becomes, like Mirandolina, the center of a comedy of her own; and many others come forward, en masse, to stand there and bicker freely in the streets of Chioggia.

Pirandello's mood here is certainly that of Shakespeare's Prospero even more than of his own Cotrone. What Goldoni gives us in the streets of Chioggia is as marvelous, surely, as the magic storm worked up by Prospero to frighten his prisoners and teach them a lesson. Ariel, you remember, reports back to his master that the charms have indeed worked wonders; the shipwrecked victims of Prospero's tempest are all huddled together, he says, so full of sorrow and fear that,

> . . . if you now beheld them, your affections
> Would become tender.

Prospero, who for the moment has only the *perception* of the opposite, replies simply:

> Dost thou think so, spirit?

But Ariel disarms him, undermining the detached, cold security of the puppet-master, by answering:

> Mine would, sir, were I human.

And Prospero replies:

> And mine shall.
> Hast thou, which art but air, a touch, a feeling
> Of their afflictions, and shall not myself,
> One of their kind, that relish all as sharply
> Passion as they, be kindlier mov'd than thou art?

The art of Pirandello's *sentimento del contrario* is to bring us where Ariel's reply brings Prospero.

I should like, at this point, to extend my discussion to illustrations drawn from Pirandello's plays. First, I must return briefly to *Liolà,* which I consider the key to Pirandello's dramatic world; I shall then touch on the relevance of my earlier remarks in the context of *Così è (se vi pare),* where paradox is embodied in the figure of Signora Ponza; and finally, I shall turn to a consideration of what is certainly Pirandello's most subtle and creative example of the concentric build-up of paradox, *Enrico IV.*

The Sicilian realism of *Liolà,* its easy and traditional structure, the recognizable types—at once characteristic and unique—may mislead us into regarding this early but unusual play of Pirandello's as a struggling toward form, as a preliminary effort of a gifted playwright not yet sure of himself. Nothing could be farther from the truth, in my opinion. *Liolà*—like Shakespeare's early but masterful *Julius Caesar*—is already a perfect expression of what will be the dramatist's peculiar idiom, his unusual and even eccentric style. Pirandello, of course, had Machiavelli's *Mandragola* vividly before him (there can be no doubt about that): *Liolà* is a romanticized aberration of that perverse and bitter redoing of Livy's story of the virtuous Lucrece. Already there is a paradox working itself to the surface in Pirandello's choice of subject. It is the same basic story as that of Livy and Machiavelli; but the perceptions and the feelings of the opposite are inspired by Machiavelli's bitter realism, adapted to a new purpose which redeems the negative, almost unbearable, Machiavellian insights into human nature. Pirandello turns things right side up and upside down again in this early work, producing some of the most complex and paradoxical characters ever to appear on the contemporary stage.

Uncle Simone is drawn undoubtedly as the modern equivalent of Nicia, but how utterly different is his comic posture, if indeed we can speak of a comic posture at all! And how completely ambiguous is his final equivocal decision to accept what Nicia in *Mandragola* unwittingly consents to accept, thinking that he has outwitted the clever *imbroglioni* who wanted to put something over on him. Nicia is comic in one of the two ways that Hegel talks about: he is comic in the eyes of the audience. Uncle Simone is comic—if at all—in his abstract role as the childless old rich man. But in the play (as we have noted) he takes on many nuances, many complex masks which suggest a secret awareness of the complexities of the situation, an internal confrontation with self which enables him to assert his intention to recognize Mita's child as his for the same reasons that enabled him to accept (for a time, at least) the suggestion that he should allow Tuzza's child to be called his. We sense, in his recognition of that paradox, a sensibility which cannot be attributed to Nicia.

What about Liolà himself? And Mita? Liolà is a seducer, we know, but not the sort of seducer that Callimaco is in *Mandragola*. He is more—let us say—"architectural" than passionate in designing his seduction of Mita. His object unmistakably is to undo the threatened harm that his earlier "seduction" of Tuzza now poses. With her plan to dispossess Mita, in effect, on the strength of Liolà's virility, Tuzza has rather seduced Liolà than been seduced *by* him. Liolà's position is paradoxical to begin with; it parallels, under the circumstances, not so much that of the young lover in Machiavelli's play as that of Fra Timoteo, on whom the responsibility falls to make all things work out for the best, as far as possible, despite the good or bad (mostly bad, in this case) motives of all involved.

In Liolà, Pirandello has created a god-image, a modern Pan who bestows his gifts with charitable abandonment. He makes girls pregnant, but there is no malice in him. He respects the societal order, the lines of demarcation between respectability and personal indulgence. The women who become pregnant are, as a rule, outside the ordinary categories. We are given to understand that there has been no confrontation, no reversal of essential values in those cases. Moreover, Liolà has taken on the children of those seductions and is raising them as his own.

Mita's case confirms those qualities in Liolà which we could only infer from what we learn of his past actions. In her case, self-indulgence is not a factor at all. Liolà adheres to all the rules of respectability in a quirky way, persuading Mita that she must counter Tuzza's selfish move by having a baby of her own by the same means. Why? Because the wicked should *not* triumph in the world; and Tuzza's plan *is* wicked. It is a case, in Pascalian terms, of *le dupeur dupé,* the Bible's deceived deceivers. Mita is surely a victim, to begin with. But in seeking her own, of course, she too takes on paradoxical attitudes. She must be selfish in order to be unselfish. She must submit to Liolà not out of personal desire, but because the essential values below the surface of respectability must be preserved. The threat she faces calls for quick thinking and action. She herself is too naive, too committed to the code of obvious respectability in which she had been raised, to take the kind of initiative Tuzza has already taken. And yet, when her very existence in the social framework is threatened—and not only hers but ultimately Uncle Simone's—she allows herself to be drawn into a new play, not unlike that of Tuzza at first glance, but in the final analysis the very *opposite* of Tuzza's both in the intention which motivated it and the urgency behind it.

Mita and Liolà are, in fact, responding with a *sentimento del contrario* to a nefarious scheme put into motion by others. There is no way out of it, except to reciprocate in kind. The paradox is in the similarity of the two plans which is, of course, a contradiction. Tuzza confesses to Uncle Simone— but to make *her* point and to gain *her* advantage; Mita does *not* confess, and in maintaining the respectable posture she preserves the essential respectability of her role as mother and devoted wife, as well as her husband's advantage. Somehow, Pirandello makes all of this quite believable and acceptable. How? By building a complex structure of seduction/non-seduction; intrigue/reaction to intrigue; human cupidity/divine, outgoing love worthy of the gods; greed and selfishness/self-protection; naive sentimentality/naive self-interest; human initiative/miraculous coincidence; and so on. Paradox is the very texture of the play—the first of Pirandello's complex dramatic contradictions which reinforce, rather than negate, the basic positive premise that ultimately it is the human *will* that structures the universe and gives it meaning. We believe; and in the assertion of that belief, the will is made strong.

But what happens when others try to shatter that belief, try to prove the will is weak? In *Così è (se vi pare)*, Pirandello tackles that aspect of the question, demolishing with the persistence of a grand inquisitor the facts as they emerge, as they are weighed and measured, as they are put forward as evidence. To me the ending of the play is predictable; what is exciting is the cumulative effect of the various sets of arguments, the spiraling toward some kind of "proof," the apparently failsafe scaffolding Pirandello builds up to shake our confidence in facts as external forces acting upon us. What an incredible series of facts, of incontrovertible evidence! And what an incredible combination of chance occurrences which seem to make that evidence foolproof!! Who can dare challenge those facts?

Laudisi, the Socratic skeptic without the Socratic assurance of inner truth, has often been called the spokesman for the playwright. On the contrary: Laudisi is the pseudo-Pirandellian, the empiricist par excellence who weighs and measures the contradictions as they surface, who delights in the purely negative role of exposure, who is not really prepared to trace the truth but insists on the preliminary leveling process of destruction, of complacent reality, of spurious facts. In that role, he is the balance which keeps the scale from tipping to one side or the other for most of the play. At a certain moment, however, skepticism must give way to something else. Pirandello builds the dramatic confrontations around the two people in the play who are truly committed, who have *willed* the truth—each according to his particular self-assertion—creating it for themselves *ex nihilo*. Two committed characters; two contradictory truths. Where does the *real* answer lie? There can be *no* answer at all, so long as the question is phrased in that way, and the answer is sought in another external *fact,* or another external combination of *circumstances*. Certainly Laudisi offers no answer. He simply dramatizes the contradictions in the play. Certainly Ponza and his mother-in-law cannot provide a *single* answer of the kind the others expect. Their positions are diametrically opposed; and yet they strike sympathetic chords which remind us that they are not very far apart in the quality of their commitment. But surely the answer may be found in Signora Ponza—the object of all the concern and all the detective work. She certainly can tell us who she is.

Pirandello drives us relentlessly from one set of facts to another and another, until there are no facts left to consult; and then, finally, he presents us with the *embodied* fact, the one person who can give us a direct answer. And here, of course, Pirandello's *sentimento del contrario* becomes dramatically immediate and visual. Signora Ponza turns out to be the ultimate, absolute paradox, the last in a series of incredible statements which are ambiguous in the same way that the oracular utterances of the Delphic priestess were both ambiguous and potentially true in an absolute way. Signora Ponza acknowledges the paradox of her own essential being by reiterating her relationships to Ponza and to Signora Frola. What is she in herself? The *certainty* of their conviction: she is Ponza's wife and Signora Frola's daughter. Reality has been penetrated and exhausted in those two assurances. As for the others who want to reach *out* instead of reaching *inside* themselves for meaning: I can only be for them (she says) an abortive fact. Even Laudisi, who undermines so completely the dichotomy of reality and illusion, nevertheless has accepted the premise of fact and fiction. The veiled woman need not unveil for the man who willfully insists she is his wife or for the woman who as willfully insists she is her daughter; but for those who still look outside themselves for direction and assurance, she can be only a clever trick, an incomplete notion, a mystery.

There is a certain humor in all this, just as there was in certain aspects of *Liolà*. There is also a great deal of irony—and not just the verbal kind we find in Laudisi or in Diego Cenci in *Ciascuno a suo modo,* but also irony of situation, particularly in the contradictory postures which the Aguzzi and their friends assume as each set of seemingly irrefutable facts comes to light. Here, as in *Liolà,* the turning of the tables carries a certain comic satisfaction; but the context is a larger, more complex one, always. The final resolution of Pirandellian laughter—even in a play like *La patente (The License)*—is always, also, full of pathos. Human compassion and pathos control laughter and direct its effects. One of the best examples of the weaving together of irony, laughter, and human pathos is *All'uscita (At the Exit),* where the drama is a series of splintered infinities, an almost allegorical setting in which half-baked ghosts must attain their one overwhelming earthly wish before they can be swallowed up into merciful oblivion. The old man (a kind of anagogical version of Uncle Simone) disappears (his walking stick falling to the ground) only after he has witnessed his unfaithful wife cry at the sight of a little boy, the child she never had and always wanted. The woman herself, just killed by her lover, runs after the cart on which the child sits—condemned, one suspects, to an eternity similar to that of Tantalus, reaching out but never grasping what she wanted most. The philosopher remains, for he will never know truth. There is a comic frenzy about this marvelous one-act play, a great deal in it that is laughable and rather wild. And yet, the total effect is powerfully pathetic in the best sense of the word. The combination of opposites can best be assessed, I think, if we compare this play with Thornton Wilder's *Our Town,* which many have said was inspired by *All'uscita.* The difference, in my opinion, rests ultimately in the subtle juxtapositions of comedy and pathos which Pirandello weaves together into a complex fabric of humor. Human emotions are stripped of all contingencies and revealed in the one true mask.

It is in *Enrico IV* that paradox, combined with the pathos of the human condition seen as tragic and humorous, is given full play and large dramatic expression. There is comedy of sorts in the masked pageant extended to a lifetime of play-acting; humor in the adjustments which the retainers have to make as they join the company before they become aware of the reality of the script they have been given to play; humor, also, in the stratification of deception, beginning with the cosmetic effort of the Marchesa to look younger and ending with the deception of portraits replaced by real, live figures in the deceptive posture of still life. Humor is present throughout the play—even in the madness of the chief protagonist, a madness which is itself a paradox, of course, since at the time of the action of the play, he is no longer mad.

Beyond the humor which rises from the individual extravagances and offbeat postures already described, there is the nervous humor of a script which cannot be fully understood on the surface of things—just as the situation in *Così è (se vi pare)* could not be fully understood so long as reality remained *outside,* experience felt as something *external* acting upon the individual like the cosmetics applied by the Marchesa to hide her age. Why does the Emperor (so-called) do what he does, live in the way he does, insist on the play-acting made real? Why is he rewriting the history of Canossa? That project in itself need not be humorous; but it is, because he is rewriting, in fact, his entire life-script and those of others around him—and in the discrepancy between the large fact and the small private cause a smile is evoked. The would-be historian becomes almost comic in the impossible task he has assumed. Almost, but not quite. There is pathos too in his effort to escape through madness or the fiction of madness; and that pathos is strengthened in us with the realization that madness has been reversed without effecting any visible change. The Emperor chose to remain embedded in his role. A sane person would not do that, would he (we might ask at this point)? But we realize the insignificance of the question in this particular context where logic and consistency are rigorously applied. And it is that fabric of logic and consistency that must be penetrated if humor is to be perfected here. Like Hamlet, the mad Emperor is not really mad; but in the same way that Hamlet assumes heightened comic effects in the play scene, where his hysterical lucidity can mislead the spectator into thinking he really *has* solved the problem of how to kill Claudius and is on the verge of doing so, in that same way the protagonist of *Enrico IV* may appear comic in his direction and production of an elaborate court play which has no reality for anyone else except himself. What a waste of energy! we are tempted to say in both cases. It is funny . . . or would be funny, if it were not so sad. It is, obviously, both at the same time.

Perhaps in Pirandello's masterpiece, as in Shakespeare's, we witness a new and unique kind of humor. In both *Hamlet* and *Enrico IV,* there are two sets of images which are never reconciled. In both, every effort is made to resolve the double image which produces fuzzy effects and makes direct purpose hard to fathom. In the protagonists there is more than the surface can ever reveal; the objective correlative is not exact, correspondences are off just a little, and therefore objects and intentions are never perfectly in focus. Pirandello's hero tells us he was ready to return to the world . . . perhaps . . . if everything had gone well—that is, according to *his* plan, *his* script. But the facts of the situation suggest, on the contrary, an impenetrable determination consistent with the earlier decision to remain isolated. Like Hamlet—who is never farther from the revenge he has promised to carry out than he is during the play scene, when he realizes that he cannot tell anyone *why* he should kill the king without sounding mad and breaking his promise to the Ghost, and that if he *does* kill Claudius he will appear to be the very same kind of usurper he has judged his uncle to be—the mad Emperor in Pirandello's play has in him, already deeply embedded, the ending of his own play. That ending is consistent with all the rest. Madness is not the question at all in *Enrico IV* (just as it is never the question, really, in *Hamlet*); it is simply one of many masks behind which the pathos of self-reflection is hidden from the world. To the rest of humanity watching the effort from a safe distance, such pathos may indeed appear comic. One could trace with profit, I think, the hysterical effort of both protagonists—Pirandello's Henry and Shakespeare's Hamlet—to come to terms with the world. The hysteria bothers us, even as we smile, or laugh.

All of us must pass through the crucible of consciousness/self-consciousness/infinite reflection of self. Pirandello, not surprisingly, talks at length and with great insight of the process of self-awareness in "L'umorismo." Toward the end of the little book, he writes:

> Let us [consider] the construction that illusion builds for each of us, that is, the construction that each of us makes of himself through the work of illusion. Do we see ourselves in our true and genuine reality, as we really are, or rather as what we should like to be? By means of a spontaneous internal device, a product of secret tendencies and unconscious imitation, do we not in good faith believe ourselves to be different from what we essentially are? And we think, act, and live according to this fictitious, and yet sincere, interpretation of ourselves.

We have in this brief passage the explication of the Pirandellian brand of humor as it appears in and through dramatic character: a necessary and paradoxical awareness of extremes. That movement takes on a variety of overtones, colors, and textures in the Pirandellian repertory, a variety which includes comedy and satire, laughter, symbolic metaphorical effects—in short, the entire spectrum of human emotions and reactions. Pirandello describes the full effects as follows:

> Reflection, indeed, can reveal this illusory construction to the comic writer and to the satirist as well as to the humorist. But the comic writer will merely laugh, being content to deflate this metaphor of ourselves created by spontaneous illusion; the satirist will feel disdain towards it; the humorist does neither: through the ridiculousness of the discovery, he will see the serious and painful side; he will disassemble the construction, but not solely to laugh at it; and, instead of feeling disdain, he will rather, in his laughter, feel compassion.

Humor is part of pathos; together they contain the full panoply of human emotions and *sentimenti del contrario*. Neither is complete in itself; in opposition they constitute a paradox; but that paradox, the heartbeat of the Pirandellian world (as also of the Shakespearean world), is ultimately one truth, one vision. In the movement from fact to contradictory fact, from extreme to extreme, from sad to happy, from certainty to doubt, that vision emerges (Pirandello reminds us at the close of his book) as a series of delicate balances:

> The oneness of the soul contradicts the historical concept of the human soul. Its life is a changing equilibrium; it is a continual awakening and obliterating of emotions, tendencies, and ideas; an incessant fluctuating between contradictory terms, and an oscillating between such extremes as hope and fear, truth and falsehood, beauty and ugliness, right and wrong, etc. If in the obscure view of the future a bright plan of action suddenly appears or the flower of pleasure is vaguely seen to shine, soon there also appears our memory of the past, often dim and sad, to avenge the rights of experience; or our sulky and unruly sense of the present will intervene to restrain our spirited imagination. This conflict of memories, hopes, forebodings, perceptions, and ideals, can be seen as a struggle of various souls which are all fighting among themselves for the exclusive and final power over our personality. . . . Life is a continual flux which we try to stop, to fix in stable and determined forms, both inside and outside ourselves, because we are already fixed forms, forms which move in the midst of other immobile forms and which however can follow the flow of life until the movement, gradually slowing and

becoming more and more rigid, eventually ceases. The forms in which we seek to stop, to fix in ourselves this constant flux are the concepts, the ideals with which we would like consistently to comply, all the fictions we create for ourselves, the conditions, the state in which we tend to stabilize ourselves. But within ourselves, in what we call the soul and is the life in us, the flux continues, indistinct under the barriers and beyond the limits we impose as a means to fashion a consciousness and a personality for ourselves. In certain moments of turmoil all these fictitious forms are hit by the flux and collapse miserably under its thrust; and even what does not flow under the barrier and beyond the limits—that which is distinctly clear to us and which we have carefully channelled into our feelings, into the duties we have imposed upon ourselves, into the habits we have marked out for ourselves—in certain moments of floodtide, overflows and upsets everything.

It is highly relevant, I think, that "L'umorismo" should end with references to Copernicus, who "disassembled . . . the haughty image we had formed [of the universe]"; Leopardi, who wrote a magnificent satire on the subject; and the telescope, "which dealt us the *coup de grâce:* another infernal little mechanism which could pair up with the one nature chose to bestow upon us." Humoristic reflection, he goes on to say, in this case—as in all cases of such reflection—suggests that we invented the telescope "so as not to be inferior." The feeling of the opposite here takes on this form . . . " 'Is man really as small as he looks when we see him through an inverted telescope? If he can understand and conceive of his infinite smallness, it means that he understands and conceives of the infinite greatness of the universe. How, then, can one say that man is small?' "

In Pirandello's dramatic universe, the progression can be measured in many ways. The detached skeptic Laudisi becomes the involved skeptic Diego Cenci and finally the vulnerable skeptic Henry IV, who would understand perfectly Hamlet's struggle with the paradox of the human soul:

> What a piece of work is a man! how noble in reason! how infinite in faculties! in form and moving how express and admirable! in action how like an angel! in apprehension how like a god! the beauty of the world, the paragon of animals! And yet to me what is this quintessence of dust?

Or the feeling of the opposite in George Herbert's Pirandellian lines:

> O what a thing is man! how far from power,
> From settled peace and rest!
> He is some twenty several men at least
> Each several hour.

It is not Laudisi but Henry IV who comes closest to identification with Pirandello himself, who wore at least as many masks each several hour as Shakespeare himself wore and graciously shared with *his* favorite and most celebrated creation: Hamlet.

GIOVANNI SINICROPI

The Metaphysical Dimension and Pirandello's Theatre

It seems that throughout history, no other art form has stimulated man's curiosity about its genesis as much as the theatre. This is certainly due in part to the fact that the composite structure of theatre allows it to appropriate almost all other forms of expression. Indeed, one might say that every other form of *poiesis*—from the lyric mode to architecture, from painting to music, from narrative to dance and even to film—may become auxiliary to the theatre. Still, the insistence with which we continually return to meditate on the origins of theatre is also due to the latent or explicit intuition in each one of us that a knowledge of its genesis would at the same time mean a comprehension of its true nature, which seems ever to elude us. There seems to be a constant temptation to explain the nature of theatre by making it derive from another form of *poiesis*, be it dance, song, sculpture or forms of lyric or narrative poetry, thus pursuing its nature in the other, in the diverse, in that which is not yet theatre but might risk becoming, by a sudden impulse or miracle, theatre.

However, in the very moment when we believe we have grasped the true nature of theatre, it eludes us once again, for that sudden impulse or miracle becomes in itself difficult to explain; what at first seems a very small gap easily bridged becomes upon closer examination a crevice impossible to span. Once again we are back at the point of departure, where all we know about the origins of theatre is what we manage to conjecture, to imagine; that is to say, the genesis, and with it the true nature of the theatre, must be

From *Modern Drama* 20, no. 4 (December 1977) © 1977 by the University of Toronto, Graduate Centre for Study of Drama.

reinvented each time, reconstructed intuitively in our imaginations and in what Vico would call "poetic criticism."

Yet one conclusion about the genesis and nature of the theatre appears certain, and seems to resist the wearing effect of the critic's file: that theatre is first of all and fundamentally a circumscribed space where an action takes place which has, among its more important properties, that of being infinitely repeatable. Obviously, this definition does not presume to attend to every critical point of view, but rather calls attention to those structures which seem to be more or less universally recognized as fundamentally specific to the theatre. By these I mean the relational functions which are established between a repeatable action on the one hand, the space in which it takes place on the other, and time, that element so difficult to embrace in a precise definition, but which here (returning to the discussion of Aristotle) may be defined as a constant value of the functions which have as their arguments either or both of the two functors space and action.

It becomes immediately clear that the elements which a structural analysis must recognize as specific to the theatre are those which classical thought from Aristotle to the Renaissance has already isolated, namely, action, time and space. All other features are variable components of one or the other of these three basic terminals. Therefore a modern analysis must not linger on the structure of the action, but rather focus all its attention on the functional relations established among the three fundamental functors; only from a careful study of these can one deduce all possible dramatic structures, and the dramatic structures in turn may account for all differences and specific features contained in the genre as possibilities. If one calls to mind plays such as *Oedipus Rex, Hamlet, Phèdre, La Vida es sueño, Faust, Six Characters, Endgame*—immediately recognizable works which are models of dramatic structures—it becomes mnemonically evident how in each of them the three fundamental elements, time, space and action, take on particular reciprocal relations which by themselves manage to sustain, indeed constitute, the particular and individual dramatic form.

If we pause for a moment before the structure of Attic tragedy, we notice that it rests on certain fundamental oppositions which concern space, time and dramatic action (plot). For example, in *Oedipus Rex* there are in fact two stories narrated: that of the destiny of Oedipus and its fulfillment; and that which relates the hero's growing consciousness of the tragic destiny assigned to his existence. The first of these two stories begins even before the birth of the protagonist and continues even after the performance has reached its end, whereas the second begins and is entirely consummated as scenic action, that is to say, it unfolds within the limits of scenic time and space. We may then distinguish two narrative levels within the "plot," the first constituted by the events forming the myth of Oedipus (the prophecy of his fate, his birth and subsequent exposure, the patricide and incest, etc.), which we shall call *fabula;* and the second consisting of events which bring Oedipus to consciousness of himself and his plight (his determination to investigate his own origins, his rebellion against Teiresias and Creon, his desire to discover the person responsible for the sacrilege against the gods, etc.), which we shall call *action*. It is clear that the level of *fabula* becomes actualized through external events, while the level of *action* is actualized only through internal events (i.e., emotions). The catastrophic *peripeteia* occurs at the moment when the chain of events from the level of *fabula* intersects with that of the narrative level of the *action:* that is to say, at the moment when the oracle is fully realized both as event and consciousness. At the point when Oedipus as well as Jocasta, Creon, the chorus—in sum, all dramatis personae—achieve awareness of the identity of Oedipus, all the connecting links of the woeful and sacrilegious tale come to light, and all the relations among the characters are restructured.

The opposition between the two levels of *fabula* and *action* is manifested through the existential co-ordinates of time and space, co-ordinates which are bound to those two levels by a relation of reciprocal interdependence, but are not, at least in Attic tragedy, parallel to them. It is obvious that the level of actualization of the *action* is that of the present, while the plane on which the myth unfolds is that of the past. Nevertheless, things are not so simple as they appear at first. In fact, the *action* unfolds along a chronological axis, and each link is tied to the next by an evident relation of cause and effect. On the contrary, the *fabula* does not proceed along the chronological axis, but its links meander from present to remote past, and the causal relation that ultimately binds them together reveals itself in the fulgurating moment when Oedipus' awareness is realized.

Furthermore, the dimension within which both levels of the plot become actualized, namely the dimension of physical space, is in turn divided into two parts, the *skene* (stage) and the *cavea* (audience), which are also bound together by a relation of interdependence. Indeed, one cannot conceive of the scenic space without that of the audience, and the latter is inconceivable without the former. Thus, even within the spatial dimension there emerges a binary opposition, which is in turn converted into an homologous opposition within the temporal dimension. The present of the *action* is not the same time, the same present, of the *performance:* the scenic present of *Oedipus Rex* has an identical value for Sophocles, Aristotle, Seneca, Racine, Pirandello, and for us today; the present of the *performance* is instead different in each case. Along the temporal co-ordinate, therefore, one must isolate two dimensions of the present: an indefinite present, infinitely repeatable; and a definite present, one and the same with the passing moment, tightly circumscribed within the *hic et nunc*, possessing, among other properties, that of being unrepeatable.

It is precisely within the limits of the *hic et nunc* that the *catharsis* takes place. I intend here to discuss not the historical content of the notion of *catharsis*, but simply its relational functions. From a structural viewpoint, *catharsis* must be seen as a functional relation that concerns the three fundamental elements of theatre, and it must be defined as a relation of solidarity: 1) between the two levels of the plot—since it results from the *peripeteia* (deriving from the acquisition of consciousness in the *action*) and the *catastrophe* (the realization of the prophecy in the *fabula*); 2) between the two dimensions of the tragic space, i.e., *skene* and *cavea*; and, finally, 3) between the indefinite present of the *action* and the definite present of the *performance*.

If this analysis has been precise and reliable, at this point we should be able to isolate in Attic tragedy two series of components: a first series disposed within the spatial-temporal dimension and constituted by the events occurring within the limits of the theatre, either those of the *skene* or those of the *cavea;* and a second series disposed beyond the boundaries of theatre, beyond scenic space and time. The result is that on the one hand, we find ourselves before a physical and sensorial dimension spatially and temporally measurable and finite, and on the other, before a non-sensorial dimension, spatially and temporally incommensurable and infinite, which we may call metaphysical.

Far from providing antecedents to the scenic action or even essential links in the chain of events constituting the *action*, this metaphysical dimension forms an autonomous series, a matrix-series upon which all the moments of the scene depend, and which, in fact, is presupposed in the very possibility of their representation. What is actually enacted on the stage is nothing other than a series of desperate attempts to evade, through rebellion, the fatal oracle which preceded Oedipus in the world. If, therefore, the dimension of *fabula* may retain its integrity without the dimension of *action*, the opposite is impossible, for the destiny understood and explained in the *fabula* represents the content of the hero's will to know. Once the entire parabola of the prophecy and the events which compose the *fabula* is unfolded, the hero must add only a gesture of consciousness at one of its links to effect his perdition. For this reason, in Attic tragedy, the *fabula* cannot be conceived as the "purport" (the "matière," the raw material) underlying the "substance" of the *action*, and therefore as its antecedent; rather it is substance already formed. The two terminals coexist in a reciprocal tension which is the very essence of the dramatic conflict.

The coexistence of the two dimensions causes a series of oppositions on several levels. On the syntactical level, for example, Oedipus appears as the subject of the occurrences within the scenic dimension of the *action*, whereas in the metaphysical dimension he appears simply as the object of an irrevocable course of events determined by fate. Along the spatial-temporal co-ordinates, the two dimensions appear anisochronous and anisotropic: in the metaphysical dimension time is not finite, but infinite; Oedipus' destiny always was and will be. Like time, space is infinite in its circularity. In this infinity, time and space are opposed in an absolute way to the coercive proportions of the tragic scene, confined to a strip of stage and one "revolution of the sun."

Consequently, the physical dimensions of the scenic space—which seem to reach their extreme limits in the case of *Prometheus Bound* or *Philoctetes*—become the iconic sign of the limits of human existence, whereas the parabola of the sky which forms the ceiling of that space becomes the iconic manifestation of the metaphysical dimension upon which the theatre, in its totality, depends. Thus, Greek theatre appears as a tragic space surrounded on its two sides by two open dimensions: one open towards the audience, the people, Greek society; the other open towards infinity. The first is an opening towards contingency, history; the second towards the eternal and unknowable. At the two ends of the tragic space there appear simultaneously the Greek people and the Greek gods. In the Greek universe, theatre thereby represents the place where the free people of Athens, that is to say the historically contingent, might, for an instant, encounter the eternal unknowable. The shudder caused by such an encounter was the true and only substance of catharsis. By means of catharsis, life could be identifiable with the tragic space. For these reasons, one may speak of theatre as ritual, and for the same reasons one may assert that Greek theatre constituted a profoundly and thoroughly social institution, national and popular.

Once the metaphysical dimension falls away, so—simultaneously—does the peculiar structure and value of Attic tragedy. It was not the Socratic spirit, as Nietzsche suspected, which destroyed the tragic spirit; it was rather the decline of the dialectical opposition between the metaphysical dimension and the tragic space. Which of these two conditions influenced the other, however, is a moot point.

When the Renaissance made attempts to reconstruct tragedy according to the *Poetics* of Aristotle, the notion which remained most difficult to comprehend and rebuilt was that of *catharsis*. The reason was that in the new theatre, the terminals of the structural function of *catharsis* were radically different. The space assigned to the theatre in the Renaissance was no longer open but closed. In the space allotted to the audience, there were not the people, but a social class, while on the other side of the scenic space there was no longer the religious power of the myth, but a literary mythology. Renaissance theatre, closed and grandiose, stable and static, was to become not a national but a state institution, not democratic but monarchic.

Renaissance and Baroque stately theatre on the whole is not the homologue of human existence but the analogue of reality on a scene in which human life unfolds in its totality. Never before and never afterwards could the theatre cover the entire gamut of relational possibilities with regard to historical life and society, from the thoroughly organic integration of comedy (with the exception of the *Commedia dell'Arte*) to the total alternative represented by great tragedy. This tragic theatre, however, rests no longer upon the tension between the physical and the metaphysical dimensions, but upon the infinite modifications of Ficinian microcosm where Prospero succumbs in his struggle with Ariel and Caliban. The unfolding of this struggle is isochronous and isotropic, and occurs in a space conceived as a sign standing for the (immanent) "Elsewhere" in its entirety. Shakespeare is able to fit on the stage even the antecedents of the dramatic action through the device of the wandering troupe's enactment of the murder of King Hamlet; that is to say, he feels the need to transfer the past in its entirety onto the present of the scene. Racine's apparently sober scene is very subtly and innumerably frequented.

In Renaissance and Baroque tragic theatre, space and time become functional elements of one common argument, the dramatic action. That is why the so-called three unities are really not indispensable to it. Fundamental to this theatre, instead, are the functional relations existing among the various components of the dramatic action. The intense poetry emerging from this theatre derives from the profound way in which the great masters succeed in analysing the conflicts consummated within the human soul. The sublime poetry of Shakespeare, for example, is like a work which illuminates each segment of the dramatic action and the significance he is able to develop from it.

But once the voices of the great poets remain silent, the analogical character of that theatre ineluctably gives way to the mimesis of the naturalist stage which narrates a one-dimensional event extending from one point to another, no longer along the axis of time and eternity, but along that of chronology. In it, the three elements of tragedy are set in complete, reciprocal equilibrium and develop parallel to one another in perfect harmony. On the fictitious space of the naturalistic stage, fallacious and inauthentic, the curtain rises at the beginning of a probable story, and punctually falls once the event has been presented and its chronological parabola has reached its end.

The spectator remains on the other side, distant and detached; he watches and is entertained, even moved. However, only his objective observation is involved, for after all, what's Hecuba to him or he to Hecuba? Inside the closed theatre there is a chasm that cannot be spanned between *skene* and *cavea*, representing two different worlds governed by contrasting principles and aspirations, each organizing reality according to reciprocally alien laws.

On Pirandello's stage, the curtain rises one instant after it has fallen on the conclusive scene of the naturalistic theatre. When Pirandello's characters appear, the real event is over, the drama has reached its end; they come on the stage not in order to perform the dramatic event or bring it to completion, but in order to explain it to themselves and to others. In Pirandello's theatre, the harmony among time, space and action reached and perfected by European theatre on the long road from the Renaissance to Naturalism is once again broken, and the three elements coexist as an anisochronous and anisotropic cluster.

What actually happens on Pirandello's scene? We may examine as illustrations two of the pivotal plays of his theatre, *It Is So (If You Think So)* and *Henry IV*.

The structure of *It Is So* rests on the appearance of the "veiled lady" in the very last scene. Through that dramatic epiphany the play assumes a cuspidate configuration and all parts converge at one central point in which this first "strong enigma" of Pirandellian theatre is inscribed. That final apparition is constantly alluded to, announced and evoked throughout the play. In this finale, the ancient and worn technique of "everybody on stage" is not only resumed but also completely renewed by the peculiar dramatic power emanating from the veiled face of the lady in mourning.

The dramatic action of *It Is So* is centred around two quests: the first concerns the identity of the "veiled lady" and runs through the play from the first scene to the last question ("No, no, madam, for yourself you must be either one or the other"), which provokes the paradoxical answer: "For myself, neither, neither! . . . I am whoever I am believed to be"; the second concerns the relations linking the "veiled lady" to all the characters in the play from Mrs. Frola to Mrs. Cini. The veiled lady's human condition is described in hieroglyphics which she will not permit to be deciphered even when faced with her husband's or her mother's cries. Locked up by the husband's morbid jealousy or, according to Mrs. Frola's compassionate definition, "because of an exclusive plenitude of love," the veiled lady is confined and inaccessible at the top floor of a gloomy tenement, defended by a sturdy iron rail from which "so many baskets hang from cords." The image suggested is that of a well—an image that, according to Pirandello himself, seems to have had a central role in his inspiration, similar to the one occupied by the image of the Saracen olive tree that could never be planted on the scene of *The Mountain Giants*.

At the bottom of the "well" is a dark courtyard where Mrs. Frola goes every day to send messages to and receive them from her alleged daughter. But the distance from that top floor is so great and the light that pours down from there so intense that Mrs. Frola is dazzled and hardly able to see her. Between Mrs. Frola and the veiled lady there are always ninety or one hundred steps which represent an insurmountable distance. Communication is possible only through those "scantly-worded notes with the news of the day" travelling in the baskets from the dark courtyard up to the dazzling mouth of the "well," from the alleged mother to the alleged daughter. Yet this communication, elusive though it may be, is a gift reserved only for Mrs. Frola, and not, for example, accorded to the nosey townspeople whose impertinent curiosity extends to the very courtyard. There they can see the dazzling source of light, the gloominess pervading the courtyard, the guardrail, the hanging baskets, but there are no messages for them. In order to communicate with the mysterious lady, the nosey townspeople must resort to town records, eyewitness depositions or court findings. When they finally insist on meeting personally with the lady, they must have the prefect summon her to appear by his authority.

On the bases of the natures of the relationships established with the veiled lady, the characters fall into two well-defined groups: on the one hand, Mr. Ponza and Mrs. Frola; on the other, Laudisi and Agazzi with all their friends and superiors. The relations among the characters are at the same time unambivalent and ambivalent: they are univalent with regard to the object of the first quest, i.e., the identity of the veiled lady; they are univalent with regard to the values of the structural function between each group and the veiled lady. These relations are organized in a hypotactic structure: the presence of the veiled lady is presupposed by the presence of Mr. Ponza and Mrs. Frola (i.e., there would be no conflict between Mr. Ponza and Mrs. Frola without the presence in the play of the veiled lady; therefore, there would be no play). By the same token, the presence of the triad "veiled lady-Ponza-Frola" is presupposed by the presence of the group Laudisi-Agazzi-and-friends. And finally (and we shall see later on why it is necessary to specify this here), the presence of the two groups on the stage is presupposed by the presence of the audience. This hypotactic hierarchy embraces the theatre in its totality and contains each element of it.

The triad "veiled lady-Ponza-Frola" forms an autonomous unit for various reasons; the three personae carry a common drama from town to town, from apartment to apartment. Clarifying their reciprocal relations means for them establishing the true identity of the veiled lady, knowing whether her real name is Lina or Giulia, whether she is Mrs. Frola's daughter married twice to Mr. Ponza, or actually his second wife. In the latter case, Mrs. Frola would simply be an intruder in the life of the two spouses, a ghost from the past not yet vanished. If, instead, the first case is true, then Mr. Ponza's existence must have been cut in two pieces at some point in his life, and the knot that ties them together is still to be unravelled or, even worse, not to be unravelled; further, his attitude towards Mrs. Frola would be as unwarranted as that towards the veiled lady. This precarious balancing on the razor's edge of an existence that either can be rationally clarified or must be thought of as founded on an irrational basis holds the three personae together in a paradoxical bond. The relations among the three personae can be described as a triangle, with the veiled lady at the vertex, and Mr. Ponza and Mrs. Frola at the opposite sides of the base. The dialectic that sustains that uneasy equilibrium must be founded again and again on the irrationality of paradox: "She has to pretend all along that she is not herself, but another, his second wife," states Mrs. Frola (end of act 1), "and I . . . oh, as for me I have to pretend I am mad." In turn, Mr. Ponza, "in order to keep up the illusion for her," has "to roar out the truth that way—as if it were madness, *his* madness" (end of act 2). Consequently, the structural relations between the two terminals of each side of the triangle can be sustained only by an unmediated act of will, which is the vital energy that Pirandello recognizes as superior to any rational force: an act of will able to re-create, after each checkmate, the relation between the base and the vertex; able to solder, after each fracture, Frola and Ponza's existences to their ontological source. The conflict, in fact, has no other development from the first scene, in which it is posed, to the last, which is thus connected to the first so that a new cycle may begin.

The clarification of the relations existing among these three personae constitutes the aim of the quest that impels the second group of characters. The quest itself is rendered necessary by the simple presence of the Ponza family in the little provincial town. If someone were to place a pair of shoes here before us, we would be forced not only to take note of the act and thereby accept the presence of those particular objects in space, but also naturally impelled to inquire about the reasons for that presence and its meaning. The presence of those objects sparks the imperative need to investigate the relations and the structural functions that constitute its reality; it creates a kind of cognitive void that must be satisfactorily filled.

One of the characters, councillor Agazzi, is unshakably convinced that bureaucratic rationality has developed the means necessary to apprehend the truth they are searching for; it is simply a question of organizing those means effectively and employing them in a systematic and careful way. The search thus undertaken is articulated in degrees, each one of them sufficient in itself to fill the void caused by the presence of a particular object and to eliminate any doubt as to its meaning. Agazzi and his friends, therefore, begin by asking for information from the persons directly involved. The cognitive void is immediately filled by the first deposition released by Mrs. Frola. In order that any doubt may be dispelled ("There seems to be something mysterious about all this," says Agazzi, expressing his last reservation at the end of Mrs. Frola's visit), Mrs. Frola's deposition need be confirmed in only one or two details. But the tranquility that has been achieved after so much pain is destroyed by Mr. Ponza's arrival on the scene. The cognitive void is reopened and once again promptly filled by his testimony. Serenity is nearly regained and, except for some details, the strange situation can now be brought back within the harmless range of normality; certainty has almost been attained. Unfortunately, the second untimely arrival of Mrs. Frola turns things upside down again. This first attempt then turns out to be a disheartening defeat; simple testimony from Mrs. Frola or Mr. Ponza is no longer sufficient to fill the cognitive void. The quest that thus far had taken as its object the relations between mother-in-law and son-in-law will from now on be directed towards the problem arising from the two conflicting depositions, i.e., the identity of the lady held prisoner in the apartment on the top floor of the gloomy tenement at the end of the town.

Act 1 ends, then, as the cognitive void turns into anguish, and the relationship binding the Ponzas appears more and more enveloped in something that escapes perception: a certain mystery that (as Mrs. Sirelli puts it at the beginning of act 2) "is going to drive all of us mad! Last night I could not sleep a wink!" However, the fallacy of direct testimonies might be overcome by pitting the so-called "hard facts" against them. But "hard facts" simply do not exist; they have been destroyed by an accident, an earthquake, a fire, or—as is suggested by Laudisi—the three members of the Ponza family "have destroyed them within themselves, within their own conscience." The search must now rest once again on the oral depositions in an effort to penetrate and break down the act of volition on which the existences of Frola and Ponza hinge. It is the strategy of Sirelli, who asks: "By putting them together, one before the other, don't you think we will be able to tell where is the false and where is the true?"

At the end of act 2, the two groups of characters crowd together on the stage in order to test the epistemological value of the principle of non-contradiction. Unfortunately, the two levels on which the search is conducted are separated by spanless distance; the dialectics sustaining the relationship among the members of the Ponza family is of an irrational nature, whereas Agazzi's heuristic depends on a scheme of formal rationalism. There can be no meeting ground between the two. Frola and Ponza once again seek refuge in their painful equilibrium, more mysterious and inaccessible than ever, well protected from any trap set by the principle of non-contradiction. There is no other expedient left but to summon by authority the prisoner to the scene in order to take her ultimate, clarifying deposition.

Lamberto Laudisi's position is diametrically opposed to that of Agazzi. His Pyrrhonism does not concern the identity of the veiled lady or the certainty of her existence, for in this case his position would be defeated the very moment the lady appeared in the last scene of the play. Nor does his skepticism concern the relationship between Ponza and Frola, whose paradoxical reality he affirms. His Pyrrhonism, of an epistemological nature, is directed only against Agazzi's heuristic methods. Laudisi is the only character who never speaks directly to Frola or Ponza: in fact, he acts only when they are absent from the stage. His attitude towards the whole affair fluctuates between a kind of subjective skepticism modelled after Gorgias ("What, tell me, please, what can we really know about others? Who they are . . . how they really are . . . what they do . . . why they do it . . . ?") and Pyrrho's agnosticism:

> MRS. SIRELLI: Why, according to you one can never know the truth!
> MRS. CINI: Should we not even believe what we see and touch?
> LAUDISI: Why yes, you can believe, madam! But, at the same time, respect what others see and touch, even though it might be the opposite of what you see and touch!
>
> (1.2)

Thus, one may happen to find certain madmen who, "without giving a care about the phantom they carry inside themselves, run after someone else's phantom, just to satisfy their curiosity! And they believe it is different!" (2.3). Laudisi's Pyrrhonism goes beyond the schemes of Agazzi's bureaucratic rationalism, which may appear to be void of ontological content. Laudisi's standpoint, quite apart from any objective or verifiable value it may have, offers him the possibility of a radical criticism of those schemes, as he sets to work trying to disorient the gentle ladies inclined to accept any interpretation of reality. During that work of disorientation, Laudisi finds amusement in private experimentation with the fallacy of Agazzi's schemes and in making a subtle parody of them. However, he never tries to disorient Ponza or

Frola, knowing well that his skepticism could never dent the irrational cer-
titude of their faith.

Perhaps Laudisi's Pyrrhonism can be explained, after all, as the result
of his own disorientation in his own search for the relations binding his
existence to its ontological source, relations which cannot be grasped and
grow ever more distant so as to become a vain appearance, a phantom:

> Yes, I know it: I say "You," and you point at me. Go on, between
> you and me, we know each other very well! The trouble is that
> others don't see you the way I see you! Then, my dear, what will
> become of you? I mean for me, here, in front of you, seeing and
> touching myself, you, as others see you, what will you become?—
> A phantom, my dear, a phantom!
>
> (2.3)

At this point, one cannot fail to notice an important peculiarity in Laudisi's
Pyrrhonism, i.e., its rationalistic nature and genesis. In fact, Laudisi is the
character who more desperately than anyone else tries to imprison reality
within the schemes of a negative rationalism. The summoning of the veiled
lady on the stage is the result of both Agazzi's heuristic and Laudisi's negative
rationalism. It becomes more and more obvious that direct contact with the
veiled lady is as necessary for Laudisi as it is for Agazzi. They both stand
on the same shaky ground: Agazzi's bureaucratic rationalism and Laudisi's
Pyrrhonism turn out to be, in the final analysis, insufficient and worthless
epistemological tools.

The spatial distribution of all the townspeople with regard to the three
members of the Ponza family can be illustrated by another triangle, whose
vertex is represented by the Ponza family (i.e., the first triangle) and on whose
base we can place, at opposite angles, Laudisi and Agazzi. Between these
two extremes, the other characters are aligned, perpetually fluctuating
between one and the other. This geometrical order in which the dramatis
personae are arranged manifests the particular structure of the so-called
"theatre within a theatre." The relational functions isolated for It Is So can
also be isolated for the two groups of dramatis personae in Six Characters,
Henry IV, Each in His Own Way, Tonight We Improvise, and The Mountain Giants. They appear also in plays such as As You Like Me, To Clothe
the Naked, and others, where this complex structure is at work in a less
apparent, more subtle way.

Therefore, in It Is So we have the first Pirandellian play that, bringing
together stage and audience, tries to destroy the aesthetic distance between
the two divisions of the theatre space. As we have already said, the audience

of *It Is So* is related to the group Laudisi-Agazzi, just as this group is related
to the Ponza family. When the veiled lady utters her last lines—"The truth?
It is as follows: that, yes, I am the daughter of Mrs. Frola . . . and the second
wife of Mr. Ponza . . . and for myself neither, neither! . . . For myself, I
am whoever I am believed to be."—the disorientation which seizes the townspeople on the stage is immediately communicated to the audience. The search
starts all over again, *in vivo,* among the members of the audience (or the
readers) who are inexorably compelled to take a position along the axis constituted by the base of the triangle and going from Laudisi's Pyrrhonism to
Agazzi's heuristic. Thus, at the very end of the representation, Pirandello
brings the spectator onto the stage. The spectator is no longer one who is
entertained or moved, remaining at the same time objectively distant from
the scene, but one who is called to participate in the action. Catharsis can
now once again assume its place in the theatre.

In the last scene of *It Is So,* the unsurmountable barrier is not the one
that separates the stage from the audience, but the one that divides the group
of townspeople from the Ponza family, and the one, even more formidable,
that divides everybody from the veiled lady. At the climax of the cuspidate
construction, the epiphany of the veiled lady reveals itself as both the source
of the characters' search and anguish, and that which assigns a different degree
of authenticity to each of their existences. It constitutes itself, in short, as
the true and only ontological source for their existence. Her presence and
her words are and must be enigmatic if they are to make sense; the veil that
hides her face must not and cannot be lifted. If it were, the radiance of her
face would not only blind Laudisi and Agazzi, but also confound Ponza and
Frola, and the Pascalian dialectical opposition between *coeur* and *raison*
would cease to sustain their freedom: "As you see, there is a misfortune here
that must remain hidden, for only thus can the remedy that compassion has
found do its work," she says. Misfortune does not touch her, to be sure,
but it touches everyone else, those that depend on her. The lady does not
descend on a chariot adorned with flowers "girt with olive over a white veil,"
as Dante's Beatrice does, among chants of "Veni, sponsa, de Libano." Here,
she descends amidst anguish and grief, and her veil must be black. Thus,
like the "vérité cachée" of Pascal, one of the authors to whom Pirandello
returns insistently throughout his works, "elle erre inconnue parmi les
hommes. Dieu l'a couverte d'un voile qui la laisse méconnaître à ceux qui
n'entendent pas sa voix. Le lieu est ouverte ou blasphème."

Misfortune is the limit that circumscribes not only Laudisi's Pyrrhonism
and Agazzi's heuristic, but also the irrational leap of Frola and Ponza. Neither
Agazzi nor Laudisi will ever be able to surpass that limit, nor will Frola and

Ponza's lunging towards the unknown lady succeed in lifting that veil and knowing that face. The identification will never occur. It transcends any attempted approximation while, at the same time, exerting an infinite and ineludible appeal.

Now, the transcendence and the limit we have been discussing are not two episodical components of the dramatic substance of *It Is So,* but rather two cardinal elements of Pirandellian dramatic form. Certainly, the epiphany of the veiled lady, i.e., her physical presence on the stage, is an exceptional moment in Pirandello's theatre, where generally the ontological source of existence hovers imminently over and beyond the scene rather than manifesting itself in it. From this vantage point, *It Is So* may be seen as the most emblematic and at the same time least problematic work of Pirandello's theatre.

The metaphysical dimension had already been theorized in the pages of *The Late Mattia Pascal,* from a vast angulation that takes into account the whole trajectory of Pirandello's works:

> "If, in the climactic moment," says Mr. Anselmo Paleari, "the very moment when the puppet representing Orestes is about to avenge his father's death on his mother and Aegisthus, the paper sky on the ceiling of the little theatre should rip, what would happen?"

Mr. Paleari himself supplies the answer:

> "Orestes would still feel the impulse to vengeance, he would still be driven by passion, but, in that instant, his eyes would look up there, to that rent in the ceiling, from which every kind of bad omen would penetrate the scene, and his arm would fall. Orestes would become Hamlet. The whole difference, Mr. Meis, between ancient and modern tragedy, believe me, consists only in that rent in that papier maché sky."

Actually, one might expect Pirandello to refer to the theatre of Racine rather than to that of Sophocles or Aeschylus, poets in whose works tragedy reaches its highest degree of metaphysical tension. However, it is in that hole in the papier maché sky, in that laceration in the ceiling of existence, that Mr. Paleari finds the source of his peculiar philosophy (which he christens with the monstrous name of "lanterninosofia" [the philosophy of the lantern]), half esoteric doctrine, half contagious disease whose syndrome is persistently pursued and analysed in the works of Pirandello. This is the very disease that both Laudisi and Agazzi contract. For them the lantern of reason will not be sufficient to illuminate the way to the top floor of the gloomy tenement at the end of town. A few years before *It Is So,* however, the lantern about which Mr. Paleari is theorizing was seen on the forehead of Ciaula, the primordial mine boy, and its weak glimmer would still lead his unsteady steps along the burrow that took him from the darkness of the sulphur mine up to the surface where he would discover the silvery light of a Leopardian moon. Another exceptional epiphany, this one perhaps announces that of the veiled lady. A few years later the feeble light of the lamp will make it possible for Henry IV to wander from one room to another of his castle.

After *It Is So,* in fact, the ontological source of existence will have no other epiphanic manifestation. The six characters will be searching for their author in vain, and equally vain will be the appeal of Henry IV to Gregory VII, the only potentate who can free him from his prison and from his all too lengthy penance. And vain will be the mother's waiting in *The Life I Gave You* or in *The Fable of the Changed Son.* In *Lazarus,* finally, the expectation will become resigned desperation and hope will be derided. Or, when it manifests itself—as in *As You Like Me*—its attire will be more Pascalian; communication and identification will be impossible. The impossibility of contact with the transcendental source of existence separates unequivocally the metaphysical dimension from the immanent one. The only content that catharsis can assume in this theatre is that of an existential checkmate. Pirandellian tragic space is once more the finite space where the infinite search on the part of existence for its ontological roots ends in total defeat.

The result of this situation is the unhinging of the naturalistic conception of tragic space and time, and a revolutionary view of their functions and of the relation between them and the dramatic action. Pirandello's tragic space has the minimum physical substance necessary to assure a place where the existential defeat may be represented, and a cathartic encounter between being and existence may be postulated. At the outset of *Henry IV,* we are told that the same setting can be thought to represent either Goslar or Hartz or Wurms, in Saxony, in Lombardy or on the Rhine. The limitations of Pirandello's scene appear still more restricted when we consider that in plays such as *It Is So, As You Like Me, To Clothe the Naked, Trovarsi,* etc., the central dramatis personae are actually guests in someone else's home: they do not have a space of their own to enact their own drama; the space in which they are immersed is alien and alienating. Pirandello, however, goes still farther: in *Six Characters, Each in His Own Way,* and *Tonight We Improvise,* he equates scenic space with the naked stage or theatre itself, i.e., with a space which, by definition, represents a continuum and derives its substance from every new performance. This equation means that any physical substance of tragic space has been wiped out or, at least, reduced to the tenuous dimension of a symbol. This tendency is pushed to its extreme degree in *The Mountain Giants*. In Pirandellian scenic space this transformation is an effect, perhaps the most ostensible, of the structural function of time. We can say that in Pirandello's theatre the relation between time and space as conceived in Attic tragedy is reversed: space becomes a functional value of the argument of time. As we have remarked above, catharsis is re-established on the modern stage the very moment when the spectator is called once again to participate in the existential checkmate resulting in the negative denouement of dramatic action. Actually, catharsis can have no other content than that deriving from that participation, intended once again as a necessary function established between the two sides of the theatre.

Hence, at least three very important effects which had been vainly sought by the Futurists are derived. The first is the elimination of the distance between the time of the action and that of the performance, or the resolution (and consequent disappearance) of the first into the second. In other words, physical time (as distinct from metaphysical) was traditionally articulated into two dimensions, that of the action and that of the performance. In Pirandellian theatre, time is instead constituted only upon one dimension, that of the performance, *hic et nunc*. It is clear that, for example, an historical reconstruction of the setting—which is so important in modern theatre from the Renaissance to Naturalism (a presentation of *Phèdre* or *Macbeth, Don Carlos* or *Saul, A Doll's House* or even *Three Sisters* out of the "time" of the action inevitably requires radical changes in the setting, action and even dialogue)—is not pertinent to the Pirandellian scene; in fact, it is damaging, so that a staging of *Six Characters* within the temporal dimension of 1921 has always a somewhat startling and ridiculous effect. Second, if physical time is to be constructed solely upon the dimension of the performance, a drastic compression of it becomes the necessary result; hence the continuity of the time-performance which incorporates even the pauses (e.g., in *Six Characters, Henry IV, Each in His Own Way,* and especially in *Tonight We Improvise,* intermissions are calculated to fit that continuity). Unity of time, consequently, becomes once again a structure of the form. The third effect is perhaps still more interesting: because of the resolution of the time of action into that of performance, the Pirandellian scene is no longer a "sign" signifying something different from itself—as is the case in modern theatre where the setting is a mere "significant" that sends back to the "original"—but instead it constitutes reality in its entirety. Only thus can contemporary theatre present itself as "living theatre."

Pirandello has been dwelling on the works of time long before he begins to devote himself in earnest to the theatre. In 1913 he presents us with a familiar landscape with figures: the Valley of Temples in Agrigento, a young English lady accompanied by the British representative in Porto Empedocle, a goatherd looking after his scanty flock, a vivacious kid springing about the ruins of the majestic monuments. The angulations from which the beholders are looking at the one and identical space linking the proud opulence of Akragas to the ruinous misery of Girgenti are diametrically opposed: to the young lady the ruins are memorable signs of an archaeological reality; to the goatherd and his animals, a shelter from the fury of rain or the canicular heat. However opposed, the two angulations converge in the mind of the narrator, himself traveller and goatherd, witness of the present and of the past. The dimension of time can bring into the one and identical space different, diametrically opposed values and meanings. Only time can offer us such a dramatically contrasting reality as that combining Akragas and Girgenti, just as time can offer the sensitive young lady, in the same reality, the joyous tenderness of the kid and the ferine bestiality of the billy goat. As the archaeologist rejects the dimension of the present in order to conquer the authentic dimension of the past, so the sensitive young lady must reject the presence of the beastly goat in order to preserve intact the image of the playful kid. Behind the space of the goatherd emerges the more "authentic" space of the archaeologist, just as behind the space of the consular billy goat emerges the authenticity of a moment of tenderness in the contemplation of the black kid.

In an analogous way, the attempted "evocations" of the space of Madame Pace's back room or of the garden in *Six Characters* (cf. similar attempts in *Tonight We Improvise, The Mountain Giants,* etc.) are possible only when space is conceived as a functional value of time.

Thus, in Pirandello's theatre the physical dimension of the *hic et nunc* (the performance) represents an unauthentic dimension which must be continually overcome by the aspiration to reconstruct a metaphysical (and not only meta-empirical) dimension of the authentic. Authenticity consists of the attempted reconstruction of the ontological source of existence. In no other play is this aspiration carried out more clearly and poignantly than in *Henry IV*.

The various components of the stage setting of *Henry IV* are in themselves symbolic of the complexity in which tragic time is structured. At the very moment when the curtain rises, the scene contains the throne room in the residence at Goslar, the portraits of the Emperor and of Matilda of Tuscany, and the two valets. Soon after one of the valets lights a cigarette. This gesture marks the present (time of the performance), as the two portraits mark the time of twenty years before, and the throne room the time around January, 1071. It seems clear that the function of the setting consists in the simultaneous presentation of those three dimensions. All other stage components are coordinated to this purpose.

Characters are divided into three units. The first is that of the "visitors," dressed in costumes of the present, bearing names of the present: Doctor Belcredi, Marchioness Matilda, Carlo di Nolli, Frida. In the course of the play, their clothes and names tend to shift from the dimension of the present to that of the remote past; they will be compelled (albeit by their own stratagem) to don the costumes of the remote past or of the masquerade. In the presence of the Emperor, their names also enter into the dimension of the remote past: the "Duchess Adelaide," the "Abbot of Cluny," the "monk of Cluny" or "Pier Damiani," the "Marchioness of Tuscany," and the fake mask of Carlo di Nolli disguised as the Emperor. Their feigned march towards the past, undertaken in the name and for the affirmation of the present, is a mockery, blind in its direction and unauthentic in its goals; it is a movement towards folly. In a second group are the "courtiers." They also have two names: in stage directions and in the presence of the Emperor, they appear as "Harold," "Landolph," "Ordulph," and "Berthold"; privately, they recognize themselves and each other by their baptismal names of the present as "Frank," "Lolo," "Momo," and "Fino." Their consciousness is that of the masquerade, the hybridization of two temporal dimensions. Their hybridism, however, lacks the dynamic energy of ambivalence; it represents a negative pole, that of candid availability (*disponibilité*) between present and past. Among this group, John (Giovanni), the old servant posing as the Emperor's amanuensis, is an exception; his sincere devotion to the sovereign spares him the unauthenticity of the courtiers' lives and a fake name. And finally Henry IV himself—the man that must be exorcised out of the past and brought forward (back?) to the reality of the present—has no other name, no clothes or costumes into which to change. By now we know that this grouping is an ever-present feature in Pirandellian dramatic form; we recognize in it the same cuspidate form we have observed in *It Is So*. By now we know that the functional relations entertained by the various groups form a thick web not easily disentangled. But we also know that beside these groups or around them there must be room left empty where the spectator may take his rightful place.

The *plot* of *Henry IV* is simple enough. Twenty years *ago* (from the performance time) at Carnival time, the members of a social club organized a riding pageantry in historical costumes. One of the young ladies decided to dress as the Marchioness Matilda of Tuscany, and a young man hopelessly in love with her decided to dress as the Emperor Henry IV. During the cavalcade, someone (Belcredi himself?) pricked the horse on which the young man dressed as Henry IV was riding, and the young man fell to the ground, hitting his head on a rock. From that moment on, he partially lost his memory, and for twelve years he lived as though he really was Henry IV, the eleventh-century Holy Roman Emperor, surrounded by courtiers and servants in a castle that his relatives had decorated as the imperial residence. Twelve years later he regained consciousness, realizing that he was still masquerading as in the cavalcade. He also realized that by now life had proceeded forward, that his friends and circumstances had radically changed, and his youth had started to wither. Leaving the castle now to go down to the city and put on the clothes of a twentieth-century man would mean simply resigning himself to bear for life the label of a madman. He decided to continue to live in the castle pretending to be Henry IV, as if he had not become conscious of his true identity.

   Now (time of the performance) the nephew of Henry IV, Carlo di Nolli, hires a psychiatrist with the aim of bringing his uncle out of his state. The psychiatrist comes to the castle with the Marchioness Matilda Spina, who twenty years *ago* had masqueraded as Matilda of Tuscany; Tito Belcredi, presently her lover; and Frida, Madame Spina's daughter and presently Carlo di Nolli's fiancée. The doctor's strategy is that of shock therapy: by presenting the patient with a living picture of himself and Matilda of Tuscany as they were dressed the day of the accident, he will obtain a traumatic shock strong enough to shatter the fictitious consciousness and replace it with a "real" one. It is an operation of exorcism that in other times would have called for the works of the enemy of Satan and now is entrusted to the charismatic hands of the twentieth-century shaman.

   The experiment fails, since the consciousness of the dimension of present time had already been regained eight years *ago*. Henry IV reveals this situation to his fake courtiers, who, in turn, reveal it to the doctor and the visitors. Now *les jeux sont faits:* Henry IV either surrenders sceptre and crown, and re-enters twentieth-century reality; or, recognizes himself as a wily counterfeiter or—from a compassionate viewpoint—a real madman. But the protagonist chooses a third course of action: responding to the pressing provocations of Belcredi, he plunges his sword into his chest and kills him. The only alternative at the present time is a self-imposed imprisonment in the castle and in the time-dimension that chance had prepared for him and he can now deliberately choose. The descent to the twentieth-century city is barred forever.

   From this brief summary, it is clear that the *fabula* is made up of events, whereas the dramatic action consists of states of consciousness, with the exception of the final blow of the sword, which is definitely an event. The

occurrence of an event on the Pirandellian stage is exceptional, and still more
exceptional is the fact that this event is "conclusive," in that it brings to a
close a series of preceding linked circumstances and carries in itself a predictable direction. Other "happenings" that may be part of the action (the arrival
of a new courtier, the sudden apparition of the two living masks, etc.)
are mere supports of the various states of consciousness. These states can
be reduced to three, coinciding with three temporal dimensions: the remote
past as the consciousness of being the Holy Roman Emperor Henry IV, in
the mind of the protagonist; the recent past as the consciousness of having
played and still playing a role or wearing a mask, in the minds of the protagonist and of the courtiers; and finally the present as the consciousness
of not being able to escape from the temporal limits of existence, in the minds
of the three units or characters who participate in different ways—the visitors
in order to affirm and accept the limits of existence, the protagonist in order
to refuse and reject them, the courtiers in order to affirm the impossibility
of escaping them.

Here, the metaphysical dimension is split into two different levels.
However, whereas the recent past is somehow linked to the present and
presupposed by it (the present situation depends, in its totality, on what happened during the cavalcade twenty years *ago*), the remote past, the dimension in which Henry IV chooses to live, is free from any relationship of
dependence or interdependence, absolutely autonomous, having been caused
by chance first and later deliberately chosen by the protagonist. Thus the
Emperor lives the first consciousness in an absolute way for the first twelve
years; in the subsequent eight years he lives the double overlapping consciousness of the remote past and of the present. It is an overlapping that
creates in the protagonist the enviable and unrepeatable situation of an
absolute freedom of choice between two existential dimensions—that of the
present:

> At the distance of eight centuries from this remote age of ours,
> so colored and so sepulchral, the men of the Twentieth century
> are torturing themselves in ceaseless anxiety to know how their
> fates and fortunes will work out!

and that of the remote past:

> Alive in the castle of Goslar, waking up in the morning, getting
> out of bed and entering straightway into the dream, clothing
> yourself in the dream that would be no more a dream because
> you have lived it, felt it all alive in you. You would have drunk
> it in with the air you breathed; yet knowing all the time that it

was a dream, so you could better enjoy the privilege afforded you
of having to do nothing else but live this dream, this far-off and
yet actual dream! [. . .] And sad as is my lot, hideous as some
of the events are, bitter the struggles and troublous the time—
still all history! All history that cannot change, understand? All
fixed forever! And you could have admired at your ease how every
effort followed obediently its cause with perfect logic, how every
event took place precisely and coherently in each minute particular!

(end act 2)

This freedom of choice was offered to him day after day and for eight years.

The meaning of the blow of the sword that seals the destiny of the protagonist consists therefore in the absolute refusal of the present as the dimension of unauthenticity and of the limits imposed upon existence:

Nobody cares to recognize that obscure and fatal power which
sets limits to our will. But I say, if one is born and one dies . . .
did you want to be born, Monsignor? I didn't! And in both cases,
independently of our wills, so many things happen we would wish
didn't happen, and to which we resign ourselves as best we can!
. . . [. . .] When we're not resigned, out come our desires. A
woman wants to be a man . . . an old man would be young again.
Desires, ridiculous fixed ideas of course—but reflect, Monsignor!
those other desires are not less ridiculous: I mean, those desires
where the will is kept within the limits of the possible. Not one
of us can lie or pretend. We're all fixed in good faith in a certain
concept of ourselves.

(end act 1)

However, it would be an extreme banality to think that the descent to the
city is impossible simply because the protagonist would arrive "hungry as
a wolf, at a banquet which had already been cleared away" (act 3), and that
therefore the dimension of remote past represents only the last refuge offered
to him. In this case, we would fail to take into consideration one of the most
important features of the tragedy.

Why, the spectator asks, why does Pirandello insist so strongly, right
at the outset of the play, that we know which Henry IV he is talking about?
If many other things are indifferent one way or another (the same scene can
represent Goslar or Hartz or Wurms, there is no precise "localization" of
the action, etc.), why then do we have to make sure we understand that we
are before the Holy Roman Emperor? The answer can be found only in the

particular condition in which the Emperor appears, summarily wrapped in "this sackcloth here," his life "all made of humiliations," curved under "the whole weight of the anathema," as a penitent Emperor waiting to be received and pardoned by Gregory VII:

> It isn't enough that he should receive me! You know he can do *everything—everything,* I tell you! He can even call up the dead. Behold me! Do you see me? There is no magic art unknown to him. Well, Monsignor, my Lady, my condemnation is really this: that whether here or there [*Pointing to his portrait almost in fear*] I can't free myself from this work of magic. I am a penitent now, you see; and I swear to you I shall remain so until he receives me. But you too, when the excommunication is taken off, must ask the Pope to do this thing he can so easily do: to take me away from that [*indicating the portrait again*] and let me live wholly and freely my miserable life. A man can't always be twenty-six, my Lady.

                                                                              (end act 1)

In the movement towards the past we see again the search for the onto-logical source of existence, a search which is simultaneously the sign of authenticity—insofar as its undertaking represents the sole justification of existence—and the sign of absurdity—insofar as it can be undertaken only as an absolute rejection of the present as representing the temporal limits of existence, the true imprisonment of being. The attempt, however, suc-ceeds only in part, and consequently does not succeed at all; for the self-imprisonment in the dimension of the remote past can never be absolute, since it carries with it the unshakable remnants of the consciousness of the present. Therefore the only way out is, once more, the paradox of an ambiva-lent condition: why is it that "I, seated at the window, cannot really be Henry IV gazing at the moon"? What is the sense of this eternal constriction that forces my existence within the inescapable limits of only one point in eternity and infinity? That is the question that the penitent Emperor is asking of Gregory, and that forms the content-substance of the catharsis.

The movement from the present (act 1) to the overlapping of the double dimension of the protagonist's consciousness (act 2) to the final violent gesture with which the Emperor seals his definitive reentering into the remote past and tries to gain liberation (act 3), is built on the isomorphic correspondence between Pirandellian tragic form and its tragic content. Before *Henry IV,* tragedy had to obey the supreme law of temporal necessity, requiring a uni-directional development of the action from past towards present or future

Pirandello is here attempting the impossible: an absurd reversal of that law and of the temporal direction of dramatic action. As any great artist, he knew that only by shattering the old structures consolidated by undefied tradition could the twentieth-century theatre develop the new ones necessary to bring forth a new message. He achieved this purpose by anchoring the form of his theatre to the metaphysical dimension, which was to remain the most vital element of the twentieth-century theatre.

The Fugitive from Life

Pirandello was particularly sensitive to criticism that the plot of *Il fu Mattia Pascal* was altogether too farfetched for any serious reader to accept it as plausible. For the 1921 Mondadori edition he included an appendix on the contradictions between reality and imagination, where he attempted to demonstrate how infinitely absurd and unpredictable life was for even the most wildly imaginative writer. While creative artists were usually expected to remain within the bounds of verisimilitude, life itself did not have to be contained by any barriers in its erratic and illogical course. For Pirandello, so-called normal life was full of excruciating situations that persons barely managed to tolerate until circumstances thrust the mirror of truth before them. When the hurt that had been held inside a person grew too agonizing, then he would be compelled to rip off the marionette-mask of his absurd existences. Living in society made puppets of individuals, of themselves and of others. The grotesqueness of life consisted in the mechanical construction of fictitious realities that would eventually be exposed in all their absurdity. According to Pirandello, his novel was no more than the imaginative revelation of the painful falseness that masked life.

As convincing proof of his novel's plausibility, the Sicilian author cited a notice in the *Corriere della Sera* for March 20, 1920, about a man named Ambrogio Casati who had visited his own grave. While Casati was serving a prison term, his wife and her lover identified the body of a suicide victim as that of Ambrogio Casati. Seven months after Casati's death certificate was issued, the wife and lover were married. It was not until early 1920 that Casati

---

From *The Mirror of Our Anguish.* © 1978 by Associated University Presses, Inc. Fairleigh Dickinson University Press, 1978.

learned of his death and subsequently placed a bouquet of flowers on his own grave. Real life then furnished Pirandello with evidence that his imagination had not carried him beyond the limits of credibility. In fact, unknown to the Sicilian author, another famous writer at the turn of the century had also composed a drama with a plot strikingly similar to that of *Il fu Mattia Pascal*; the source for that play had been a real-life trial in St. Petersburg that involved a case of bigamy, in which a complacent husband had simulated suicide so that his wife could remarry. Tolstoy's drama *The Living Corpse* bears such a strong resemblance to Pirandello's third novel that many critics and scholars have assumed that Tolstoy based his play on the Russian translation of *Il fu Mattia Pascal,* but the date for the composition of the Russian drama was 1900. Real life, whether in Russia during the last decade of the nineteenth century or in Italy at the time of the First World War, provided examples of the absurd measures that individuals would take to escape the pressures of existing in a structured society. Both Tolstoy and Pirandello sought to protray the grotesque deformation of modern life. A third similar but admittedly fictitious case of identifying a corpse as that of one's spouse occurs in the first Italian grotesque drama, Chiarelli's *La maschera e il volto* of 1916; in that play Count Paolo Grazia has been forced by foolish vanity to pretend that he has thrown his faithless wife into Lake Como, whereas in truth he has banished her to exile outside Italy. Shortly after his court acquittal the count must make a legal declaration identifying as the remains of his wife a corpse that was retrieved by some fishermen from the lake. All these authors—Chiarelli, Pirandello, and Tolstoy—point out that life in society is an increasingly complex series of bureaucratic and judicial procedures that the individual can never truly succeed in eluding. Their grotesque art is the accurate mirror of life's absurdity.

The technique of the first-person interior monologue creates the impression of an autobiographical confession. Mattia Pascal is forever speaking to another, who might take the form of some casual acquaintance or of a curious passerby who happens to observe the librarian placing flowers on his grave. The narrator-protagonist feels constantly compelled to justify his past actions. Sometimes he will say to himself, "How do I know this?", and then he will proceed to give an explanation for his strange behavior. Mattia Pascal claims to be writing his memoirs with the assistance of the librarian Don Eligio Pellegrinotto, a person who is always trying to bring order out of chaos, whether in Miragno's decaying library or with the facts of Mattia's three lives. Since this Pirandellian novel is a book of confessions, it must be placed as a fictitious successor to a long Western tradition of confessional literature that goes back to St. Augustine and reaches a high point with Rousseau.

Because of the way *Il fu Mattia Pascal* represents a deliberate attempt to demolish the form of confessional literature, it anticipates Svevo's *La coscienza di Zeno* of 1923. Svevo wished to show how all literary confessions were fundamentally dishonest, inasmuch as the conscience-stricken authors carefully selected the episodes in their past and ended by detaching them in an unnatural and distorted fashion from the continuous stream of vital experiences. The narrator of *La coscienza di Zeno* forever lies to himself, his analyst, and the readers of his diary about the utterly selfish nature of his motives and the insincerity of his desire to renounce sensual pleasures. Although Mattia Pascal's confessions are not conscious or unconscious lies, the vision with which he surveys the incidents in his various lives is humoristic, since the narrator no sooner makes an assertion than he at once begins to dismantle it with his cold reflection. All life is seen as lacking in substance, and thus the protagonist chooses isolation. The novel opens with an admission of life's uncertainty: "The only thing I knew for sure was that my name was Mattia Pascal"; and it comes to a desolate close six months later, after the narrator has finished the work of his memoirs by declaring: "I am the late Mattia Pascal." Novelistic first-person narration in *Il fu Mattia Pascal* serves to advance the humoristic investigation behind life's provisional forms. It is indeed no surprise that Pirandello dedicated "L'umorismo" to Mattia Pascal the librarian.

Mattia Pascal is both actor and spectator in the novel. During his two years as Adriano Meis he is especially restricted to observing the life of others. Pirandello takes advantage of the protagonist's physical restrictions to focus on important figures in the work. After an eye operation, Meis must remain for forty days in a darkened room. During that period he has various guests, as on one evening a séance is held in his room. All he can discern in the dim light are outlines, and he must rely more on nonvisual impressions, such as tone of voice, than on what he is able to see. By listening to the half-Spanish, half-Italian jargon of the girl, Pepita Pantogada, he correctly judges her to be a willful and contemptible creation. Later, when Meis beholds the girl in full light, her stunning beauty so distracts him that he briefly forgets her inferior moral qualities. The author has artfully related psychological reaction to Meis's physical restriction.

Another example of Pirandello's technique of the restricted point of view can be found in the eleventh chapter, "Di sera, guardando il fiume" ("In the Evening, Looking at the River"), where Meis encounters his arch-enemy, Terenzio Papiano, for the first time. One night, when he is in his room reading, he hears voices outside on the balcony of the rooming house. At first all he can make out are the voices of a man and a woman. His curiosity (and that of the reader) is aroused when he discovers that the man's voice is not that of his landlord, the only male in the rooming house besides himself. The entire scene is relayed by what Meis can hear and see through the shutters over the window of his room, which looks out on the balcony and the Tiber. That rather brusque technique of first introducing a character with a *macchietta* type of portrait is abandoned here as the author avoids physical details to focus on the inner qualities of the strange man on the balcony and his relationship to the dwellers in the rooming house. Meis comes to realize the hold that the stranger exerts over the roomer Silvia Caporale, who submits to the man's cross-questioning and allows him to address her with the familiar pronoun. Meis is now able to learn that the man's anger and agitation have to do with the presence of the new roomer (Meis himself) in the building; the hostile attitude of the stranger threatens to destroy the precarious vital invention that the late Mattia Pascal has created for himself. In his excitement Adriano Meis pays attention to details like Signorina Caporale's putting her hand on the man's shoulder only to be rebuffed by him. All of the scene's intensity and anxiety is heightened when the intruder orders the Caporale woman to fetch the landlord's daughter Adriana from bed. The protagonist's long wait by his shutters for the appearance of Adriana Paleari on the balcony adds to the sense of dread that the stranger's arrival has caused him. The dialogue scene when Adriana does finally come is extremely short: the intruder peremptorily orders Signorina Caporale to bed and starts to interrogate the girl. After the man seizes the girl by the arm, Meis is no longer able to restrain himself and slams the shutters. Adriana calls him to the balcony. To his further astonishment, he sees a young man with a rather idiotic expression on his face coiled on a trunk in the hallway; he surmises that the youth must be Papiano's brother. Out on the balcony the stranger ceases his angry inquiry and assumes a deceitfully smiling countenance when he is introduced as the husband of Adriana Paleari's recently deceased sister. All of Papiano's basic character traits have been presented already through the protagonist's physically limited area of vision: his irritability, his disregard for the feelings of others, his ability to simulate friendliness when necessary. The mood of the scene is that of a sinister intrusion. Although the true stranger in the Paleari household is Adriano Meis, the regular dwellers like Signorina Caporale and the landlord's daughter seem to welcome him, while they fear Papiano. This technique of constructing a character portrait through suspense-filled degrees of a limited point of vision and by setting a pervasive mood partake of the same impressionistic method that Joseph Conrad employed in his novels and tales.

For many of the readers who followed the installments of Pirandello's third novel in the *Nuova antologia,* the work must have seemed like a romantic story of evasion from the responsibilities of everyday life. Mattia Pascal's disguise as Adriano Meis does indeed constitute a story of the challenges and difficulties that an individual must face and overcome after he has chosen to be a walking invention of pure imagination. The novel can thus be appreciated as merely a series of hurdles that the protagonist surmounts; the reader's interest is sustained by the vicarious thrill of seeing how each new complication is solved. As such, *Il fu Mattia Pascal* would be no more than an example of escapist literature, elevated perhaps to a metaphysical dimension by the author's humoristic concern to expose the fictional basis of social existence. There is, however, a profoundly human dimension to the novel, since it is an exhaustive study of the impossibility of an individual's forging a life that is wholly his own, independent of the sentiments of others and the institutions of modern society. Through carefully limited focus and the forever-questioning technique of interior monologue, the author probes the worlds of Mattia Pascal and Adriano Meis and determines the tormenting reasons why the protagonist must die twice, only to accept the nonlife of withdrawal to a dilapidated library. The novel thus relates to the investigation in Pirandello's tales and later plays of the contemporary alienation from inauthentic society.

THE WORLD OF MATTIA PASCAL

Since one of the protagonist's eyes persists in squinting, his entire view of the world is conditioned by defective vision. The description he gives of himself is something of a *macchietta,* emphasizing how a red curly beard has crowded his face to the disadvantage of his tiny nose. Like the anti-heroes in Svevo's novels, Mattia Pascal displays ineptitude in meeting practical problems. As a child he never paid attention to the lessons of his tutor, Del Cinque, who abandoned the effort to educate the Pascal brothers and had even borne the insulting nickname "Pinzone," taken from his pointed beard. While their saintly, widowed mother retreated to three rooms in the family's townhouse, the Pascal boys had thoughtlessly invaded the deserted rooms and roamed through them as if in so many immense chambers of experience. In his childhood Mattia did not appreciate the apparently lifeless mansion, but after he was cheated of his patrimony, he never tired of recalling the antiques, faded tapestries, and upholstery with their musty odor, as well as the deathlike stillness of the furniture. During his fugitive years as Adriano Meis, moving from one hotel to another, the image of the family mansion with its familiar objects kept on returning to his mind, like the picture of a lost paradise where he could find identity. But in truth Mattia Pascal did not realize how precious his home was until after it was irreparably lost. An American author, who has considered the importance of place for her own fictional characters, affirms that sensitivity to place indicates a depth of personality:

> There may come to be new places in our lives that are second spiritual homes—closer to us in some ways, perhaps, than our original homes. But the home tie is the blood tie. And had it meant nothing to us, any other place thereafter would have meant less, and we would carry no compass inside ourselves to find home ever, anywhere at all. We would not even guess what we had missed.
>
> (Eudora Welty, "Place in Fiction")

Pascal, as Adriano Meis, was to search in vain for a second spiritual home. But the character portrait that Pascal makes of himself in his first life is anything but flattering: a fatuous youth, utterly spineless, self-indulgent, and not particularly sensitive to others' longings or to the special setting that would remain his one true spiritual home.

Life in Miragno comes to the reader as perceived by Mattia's twisted vision. It resembles the same stagnant environment as in *L'esclusa* and *Il turno*, and it has the identical effect of deforming those who are condemned to remain there. The dramatic situation in Miragno is reduced to one of survival—but not survival against the forces of Nature as in Verga's agrarian society; rather, survival against the duplicity that corrodes the very quality of life. For Pirandello, in contrast to a writer like Hemingway for whom place is never hostile, the setting as well as its inhabitants is frequently malevolent. Those who fail to cope with the environment are condemned to perish in it, as does Mattia's mother, who loses her vast estate to her trusted administrator. Only one member of the Pascal family understands how to create a successful social role in that provincial world where mendacity and self-interest prevail: Mattia's brother Berto, who uses his good looks and fine manners to live on the dowry his wife brought him, even though his victory involves cutting off every warm sentiment toward his mother and brother. On the periphery of the Pascal family stands paternal-Aunt Scolastica, the man-hating old maid who tried to awaken the widow Pascal to her adminis- trator's disloyalty; yet the aunt was not motivated by genuine affection but merely by determination to defeat a thief. Of all the characters, Aunt Scolastica shows the greatest awareness of social role as the normative pat- tern of behavior; propriety, inflexibility, demanding that everyone should fit into a rigid scheme of correctness. While Berto seeks the appearance and privileges of status, Scolastica asserts the obligations of position. The rest of the inhabitants of Miragno exist as creatures of habit and unexamined belief, constituting an inelastic society. In Mattia's distorted sight, the memory and sometimes the spectacle of place might soothe the pain of living, but the human environment always causes suffering.

Battista Malagna, the estate administrator, emerges triumphant in that shallow world by seeking only his own advantage. His is a dynamic ethic that appropriates everything in its grasp to itself. Malagna is an individual for whom *bontà* (kindness, or goodness understood as doing something to benefit another person) would be an alien term without significance. As throughout the novel, this figure is seen through the eyes of Mattia Pascal, who has every reason to depict him as the mole who undermined the very ground upon which the Pascal fortune was founded. Whenever he speaks of Malagna, the narrator employs descriptive terms to suggest a kind of oozing, amorphous creature that spreads over everything that comes near to it:

> All of him slid down; his eyebrows and eyes slid down here and there on his long, broad face; his nose slipped down on his stupid moustache and goatee; his shoulders sagged away from the back of his neck; his enormous, loose paunch hung almost all the way down to the ground. Since his paunch fell so heavily over his short legs, the custom tailor was forced to cut his trousers with so much slack at the waist that from a distance it seemed that Malagna was wearing a very long skirt or that his paunch stretched all the way to the ground.

To Mattia Pascal this hateful caricature of a man should at least correspond to his own story-book image of a consummate thief. In addition to the exterior portrait, Pirandello presents something of the inner life of Malagna in his relationship with his first wife, Signora Guendolina, whose social class is higher than his. Malagna's autonomy comes to an end through his tyrannical wife, who constantly reminds him of his inferiority, and he rather resembles an Italian Georges Dandin in his endeavor to win acceptability by imitating the ways of the gentlemanly class of Signora Guendolina. He is not even permitted to eat and drink as he pleases, for his wife suffers from a stomach ailment caused by truffle croquettes and wine. Both husband and wife end by abstaining from wine in public while drinking it in secret. Pirandello's novel points out how even a victor in life's shabby affairs such as Battista Malagna is checked in his relations with others and compelled by his interpersonal limitations to play a charade.

The baseness of life in Miragno is perhaps best exemplified by an episode in the fourth chapter where the protagonist relates the one successful act of revenge he has committed against the thief. Malagna grieved that he did not have an heir to receive the fortune he had stolen from the Pascal family, and shortly after Guendolina's death he married a peasant girl, Oliva Salvoni, who had once cared for Mattia and expressed indignation at the administrator's acts of thievery but was prepared to wed for financial security. As the years passed, however, no heir was born; and Malagna started to abuse his wife. The old man also began to frequent the home of a distant relative of his, the widow Marianna Dondi-Pescatore, who had a rather attractive daughter, Romilda. Malagna hoped to prove his virility with Romilda, and the widow Pescatore was willing to prostitute her daughter to her own venal interest. The name *Pescatore* means "the fisher," and indeed the widow uses Romilda as bait. Mattia would never have become involved with Romilda if it had not been for the admiration that his friend Mino expressed for her. The entire relationship of Mattia-Mino-Romilda is a classic case of mediated desire. Mino has no true personality of his own: with Berto he played a Dandy; with Mattia he performed as an idiotic adventurer. Living as a submissive shadow of one or the other of the Pascal brothers, Mino seemed, with his adulation, a ridiculous figure. Yet it was a comment of his about Romilda that ensnared Mattia in a course that led to his marriage. Mattia decided to visit the Pescatore home, where he at once observed the contrast between the tattered older pieces of furniture and the gaudy additions that must have come as gifts from Malagna. After Pascal reported his favorable impression of Romilda to Mino, his friend's interest incited in him a passionate desire to have her. Romilda herself in the novel gains her only identity from her suitors or her overbearing mother; she is an evanescent figure with sorrowful green eyes and a luminous complexion. By contrast, her bony, withered mother possesses a fierce personality and spiteful temper in her own right. It was the old woman who cast the net that trapped Mattia. She left her daughter alone with the silly young man one afternoon when they were out picnicking, and Mattia succumbed to Romilda's appeal for his protection. Soon the news came out that the widow's daughter was expecting a child by Malagna, who was only too eager to have an heir. Realizing that he had been made a dupe, Mattia took his revenge by visiting Oliva and providing her with an heir. Once Malagna was sure of having a child, he publicly denied any intimacy with Romilda. Unfortunately for Mattia, the vengeance scheme backfired on him and he had to marry Romilda. This story of cuckoldry goes back to Italy's novella tradition of the *beffa,* a joke played on elderly husbands by young wives and virile lovers. Along with the Boccaccian tradition, a similar situation can be noted in Machiavelli's play *La mandragola* (*The Mandrake*), where a young lover makes it possible for an impotent lawyer to have a child by his beautiful wife. Pirandello himself used the basic plot situation of this episode in his later Sicilian play *Liolà* of 1916. The fact that the events occur in Miragno illustrates the meanness, stupidity, and hypocrisy at the core of the provincial world. One person appropriates the values of another so that everyone ends impoverished. Those who weave schemes often turn out to be victims. The joys of intelligent contrivance and sensual delight, which characterize the source of the episode in Boccaccio and Machiavelli, disappear in Pirandello's novel, with its bitter revelation of the deceit behind social relations.

All the futility and ignorance of Miragno finds its concrete symbol in the Boccamazza Library, where Mattia had to work for two lira a day to supplement the widow Pescatore's meager pension. None of the citizens make use of the library, which slowly crumbles with its accumulated years of dust. Pascal soon discovers that a major part of his responsibilities is to chase the rats—the only creatures that devoured the volumes in the building. The books sit covered with mildew, gradually disintegrating. The library's dilapidated condition and the townspeople's indifference to the deterioration of its volumes reflect the failure of civilization in Miragno's society. Sometimes the dampness that invades the building causes rather strange matings of volumes, as when the binding of a saint's life becomes attached to a treatise on the art of seduction—saintliness and lasciviousness are both extreme forms of vital commitment, such as could never be attained in Miragno's mediocre climate. Housed in a deconsecrated church, the Boccamazza Library is a shrine to absurdity.

Anyone who works in the library eventually surrenders to its deadly immobility. Although Pascal was hired to succeed the aged librarian Romitelli, the elderly man could not comprehend the reality of his retirement and continued to arrive at the library every day at precisely the same hour that he had done for years. Romitelli illustrates the two levels of comic and humoristic. Hobbling along on two canes that made it look as though he had four legs, the old man was deaf and nearly blind; but he persevered in his "work," which consisted of reading historical dictionaries and attempting to remember their contents. Libraries are places where persons should read, and in the absence of interested townspeople Romitelli assumed the task of reading as a moral and intellectual obligation. The meaninglessness of the old man's methodical, clockwork routine makes of him both a ridiculous and a pathetic figure. After Romitelli died, Mattia was forced in his absolute isolation to turn to the books to distract himself from thoughts of his domestic problems. Compared to Romitelli and Pascal, the autodidact in *La Nausée* who tries to master all the knowledge in the Bouville library according to alphabetical order appears a positively constructive figure. Because the Miragno library was threatening to transform him into another Romitelli, Pascal was partly motivated to flee the town in order to escape the building's atmosphere of decay. In truth, the essential bleakness of Pirandello's third novel results from the fact that Mattia Pascal does resume his work at the library, helping Don Eligio catalogue the texts that no one wants to read. It is in the library that Pascal composes his memoirs, which he intends to leave to the Boccamazza Foundation with the provision that they are not to be opened until fifty years after his third and definitive death. The message, then, of his three lives is to be preserved in a building that stores useless information.

Even before Mattia Pascal fled Miragno and took the alias of Adriano Meis, there were unmistakable signs of that inner conversion which often characterizes confessional literature. The entire first part of the novel is a deliberate depreciation of temporal life, wherein the protagonist has suffered the fall from an existence of ease to one of poverty and degradation. Through viewing the silent, uncomplaining agony of his mother as she huddles in a corner of the Pescatore home, Mattia ceases to be the self-centered ignoramus that he has been; he is growing aware for the first time in his life of the torment that persons can hold within themselves. One day an explosion takes place in the widow's home when Aunt Scolastica arrives to take Mother Pascal away from that hateful place. Before she leaves, the aunt succeeds in plastering Widow Pescatore's face with a roll of wet bread dough. The Pescatore woman turns her anger on her son-in-law and pelts him with pieces of dough until she collapses on the floor from the fury of her emotions. At that moment Pascal has his first genuine flash of illumination:

> I can say that since then I have been able to laugh at all my misfortunes and at every torment of mine. I saw myself, at that moment, as an actor in the most foolish tragedy that one could ever imagine: my mother running away with that mad aunt of mine; my wife in the next room in her [pregnant] condition . . . ; Marianna Pescatore there on the floor; and I who could not provide bread for the next day's meal—I stood there with my beard covered by dough, my face scratched and dripping with what was either blood or tears caused by my convulsive laughter. I went to the mirror to find out the truth. There were tears, but I was also scratched all over my face. Oh, how pleased I was with my eye at that

moment! In its desperation the eye was more determined than ever
to look wherever it wanted to on its own account.

Two major Pirandellian themes are presented in this episode: life as an imi-
tation of the stage and the mirror confrontation. Although Mattia employs
the word *tragedia*, he devaluates its starkness with the superlative form of
the adjective *buffa* to stress the comic absurdity of his domestic situation.
His experience is to see himself living (*vedersi vivere*), which actually results
in a momentary detachment of the conscious self from the stream of life's
turbulent events. Not only does the mirror reveal his abject condition, but
it also attests to the constantly distorted vision caused by Mattia's cockeye,
which asserts its independence even at times of the most intense anguish.
Mattia Pascal has been permitted to see the ridiculousness of his roles as husband and son. The earlier Pascal was in effect blind to everything around him.
This glimpse of the truth marks the first step in the protagonist's conversion.

As often in Pirandello's works, it is a death watch that precipitates events
that might otherwise be slow in developing. The firstborn of Mattia's twin
daughters died before he could feel a strong affection for her, but the second
child survived for almost a year—long enough for her father to make the
girl the sole purpose of his life. Within a period of nine days Mattia Pascal
suffered the torture of double death watches, as he kept running back and
forth from his home to Aunt Scolastica's in alternate vigils by the bedside
of his daughter and mother. The mother's death severed a fond link with
the past, while the girl's passing shattered any hope for the future. Both died
on the same day, almost at the same hour. As part of his confession Mattia
Pascal admits that his immediate reaction to the double deaths was simply
to fall asleep. The exhausting torment of the two vigils prevented him from
experiencing the grief which, when it came after he had rested, almost drove
him to insanity with its fierceness. With no past or future, Mattia Pascal had
only the disconsolate emptiness of the present. Not possessing a reassuring
belief in an afterlife in which his mother and child could know the happiness
that was denied them in human society, Pascal stood on the brink of suicide.
Yet, instead of committing that fatal act, the protagonist took advantage of
a series of chance happenings to kill not himself but the fictitious reality he
had been compelled to endure in Miragno.

OLGA RAGUSA

Early Drama

Pirandello's shift from narrative writer to playwright occurred in close connection with the Sicilian dialect theatre. It will be our purpose now to analyse
what effect this connection had, and to justify the contention that failure
to understand his Sicilian plays properly obscures the most important link—
more important even than "L'umorismo"—in the history of his development.

"Who are they? Where did they come from? How did they become such
vigorous and original artists?" With these words the drama critic of the Rome
daily *La Tribuna* on 3 December 1902, opened his review of an unusual
theatrical experience that had taken place at the Teatro Argentina. The
occasion was a benefit performance for the flood victims of the town of
Modica in southern Sicily. Giovanni Grasso (1873–1930) and Marinella
Bragaglia (1882–1918), members of two well-known Sicilian families of
actors, staged a double bill: *Cavalleria rusticana* and *I mafiusi,* the latter
replaced on the second evening by *La zolfara. I mafiusi* and *La zolfara* have
recently become available to the general public through their inclusion in
Alfredo Barbina's anthology, *Teatro verista siciliano* (Bologna 1970). They
can help us to define the kinds of plays in the repertoire of Sicilian acting
companies at the turn of the century. *I mafiusi,* recognized as the earliest
work of Sicilian *verismo* in the theatre, is the work of two itinerant Sicilian
actors, Gaspare Mosca (b. 1825) and Giuseppe Rizzotto (1828–95). Based
on the true-life experiences of prison inmates at the Carcere della Vicaria
in Palermo, it was first performed in Palermo in 1863, and thus belongs to
the first generation of the tradition with which we are dealing. It is an episodic,
confusing and difficult-to-follow play even in the Italian version which was

From *Luigi Pirandello.* © 1980 by Olga Ragusa. Edinburgh University Press, 1980.

first published in 1885. *La zolfara,* on the other hand, the work of Giuseppe
Giusti Sinopoli (1886–1923), is a conventionally constructed three-act drama
concerned with that recurrent subject of late nineteenth-century Sicilian
literature: conditions of life in the sulphur mines. First performed in Messina
in 1895, it is built around the conflict of interests between mine-owners and
managers on one side and workers—*picconieri* and *carusi*—on the other, and
is reminiscent in its sympathies and indignations of other similar works by
socially conscious naturalistic writers, such as for example the German
dramatist Gerhart Hauptmann (1862–1946). It belongs to the second generation of modern Sicilian dialect drama.

What impressed *La Tribuna's* reviewer most about the performances of
Giovanni Grasso and Marinella Bragaglia were the company's "human sense
for drama" and its "disdain for theatrical make-believe"; the fact that, in its
natural dialect, *Cavalleria rusticana* appeared more "rapid and concise," with
"flashes of fire that strike the spectator"; and the carefully orchestrated scenic
action of *La zolfara,* "thought out in every movement, in every detail,
reproducing the intense thrust of every passion as it reveals itself in different
temperaments." As for the actors, the reviewer commented upon Marinella
Bragaglia's Santuzza, "an unusual Santuzza, devoid of all artifices," and on
the "forcefulness and originality of Grasso," whom he defined "a dramatic
temperament that entrusts itself to nature alone." Naturalness, passion,
authenticity—these traits appear as well in Capuana's remarks, which can
be usefully quoted here, apropos two interpretations of the role of Santuzza,
one by the great Eleonora Duse, the other by an unidentified Sicilian actress.
In the preface to his *Teatro dialettale siciliano* (1911) we read: "I remember
two performances of *Cavalleria rusticana.* . . . In the one Eleonora Duse
played the role of Santuzza. . . . It was in the now distant days when she
triumphed by dint of her youth and the power of her art. In the other the
role was played by a poor, provincial actress wandering with her company
of four or five strolling players (*guitti*) from one inland town to the other.
. . . To my Sicilian eyes Santuzza-Duse appeared as a kind of falsification
of Verga's passionate figure in her gestures, the expression of her voice, her
dress (an unbelievable medley of Lombard and Roman costumes!), in spite
of the passionate response which only Duse could elicit. The poor, regional
actress, instead, her clothes borrowed from the peasant women of the town
she was passing through—shoes, earrings, skirt, the blue cloth cloak—became
a real, live "Santuzza," as there may have been one among her audience."

Two one-act plays, *La morsa* and *Lumìe di Sicilia,* performed on a double
bill, 9 December 1910, marked Pirandello's debut as a dramatist. *La morsa*
probably goes back to at least 1892, but *Lumìe di Sicilia* was expressly writ-

ten for the occasion or, more precisely, was adapted for the stage from the short story of the same title (1900). The plays were staged by Nino Martoglio (1870–1921), poet, journalist, dramatist, director, a close friend of Pirandello, co-author with him of *'Avilanza* (*La bilancia*, 1917) and *Cappiddazzu paga tutto* (*Cappellaccio paga tutto*, 1917), and co-author with him and Musco of the enormously successful *L'aria del continente* (1915; published under Martoglio's name alone). In the obituary written on his tragic death, Pirandello compared the importance of Martoglio for Sicily to that of Di Giacomo and Russo for Naples, Pascarella and Trilussa for Rome, Fucini for Tuscany, and Selvatico and Barbarani for Venetia, thus, incidentally, providing a capsule survey of the most important regional, dialect writers of the period. But in spite of their being "Sicilian" in subject matter and their being staged by a Sicilian impresario intent on giving Sicilian regionalism national diffusion and exposure, at their first performance *La morsa* and *Lumíe di Sicilia* were in Italian. As a matter of fact, in an article published in 1909, "Teatro siciliano?," Pirandello expressed scepticism with regard to the viability of Martoglio's ideals and rejected the contemporary Sicilian dialect theatre as it was being represented by Giovanni Grasso and Mimí Aguglia (b. 1884): "la terribile, meravigliosa bestialità" of Giovanni Grasso repelled him, and the Sicily that Grasso typified was for him unauthentic and manufactured for "foreign" consumption.

The Sicilian actor who took credit for breaking through Pirandello's resistance to the stage and literally "forced" a play out of him was Angelo Musco (1872–1937), Grasso's almost precise contemporary. The play was *Pensaci, Giacomino!* (1906), no *novella sceneggiata* (dramatized short story) this time but a work written directly for the stage, written with a specific actor in mind, and written moreover in Sicilian. The year before, in Catania, Musco had acted in a Sicilian version of *Lumíe di Sicilia*, but that play had not been written for him. Born in Catania, cradle of the Sicilian veristic theatre, Musco had begun his career as an actor by being a "voice," the voice of the *pupi* of the regional marionette theatre. By 1915 he had his own company and was developing a repertoire which included Fausto Maria Martini's *Ridi, pagliaccio!*, Capuana's *'U paraninfu*, Martoglio's *San Giovanni decollato*, Bracco's *Sperduti nel buio,* Giacinto Gallina's *Me figghia, L'aria del continente,* and a number of Pirandello's plays. In the strict distribution of parts which typified acting companies such as his, Musco was cast as the *brillante* (Pirandello's "raisonneur") and not as the *primo attore*.

What kind of performer was Musco? What was it that convinced Pirandello to entrust a number of his works to him, while, according to Giudice, he had at first felt alienated by that insistent, gesticulating, rumbustious individual who had invaded his study? "He is irresistible," wrote the drama critic Renato Simoni. "He possesses the secret, which few have, of causing laughter. . . . He is all instinct, with his fiery eyes, his sun-burnt face, his devilish mischief, as colourful as an ancient mask." "Most of the time he doesn't even have to say a word," wrote another critic, Eugenio Cecchi. "His legs speak for him . . . his shoulders . . . the folds of his suit . . . the brim of his hat." E. Gordon Craig called him simply "the greatest actor in the world." André Antoine said that he had never seen on any stage such an overflowing of sheer comic energy. Writing from a wider perspective, Silvio D'Amico, day-to-day reviewer but also drama critic and historian, noted shortcomings as well: "His fatal insubordination, his congenital infidelity to the text, his physical need to betray it and remake it, improvising evening after evening, never allowed him to become what is called an 'interpreter.'" Never allowed him, that is, to subordinate his personality to that of the play's author. In other words, Musco was a great actor in the sense that members of a *commedia dell'arte* troupe are great actors, best suited to working under the conditions of maximum freedom offered by a *scenario* rather than a *script*. He was the character, in a way similar to the Father's being a character when he brings his lived, unwritten story to a company of actors (*Sei personaggi*) or to the actors' wanting *to be* (and not to play) their parts in *Questa sera si recita a soggetto*.

It may seem strange that Pirandello, who became so punctilious, so intransigent about the performances of his plays that he did not rest until he had formed his own company and built his own theatre so that they could be performed as he desired them to be—or, as he might have put it, as they desired themselves to be—should ever have accepted a "collaborator" as unreliable, as undisciplined and independent as Musco. Many amusing and revealing anecdotes are told about their association. One concerns the dress rehearsal of *Liolà:* Pirandello, outraged that the actors had not yet learned their parts, walked off with the script and called off the performance. Musco ran after him: "Professore! è inutile che si porti il copione. Stasera lo recitiamo a soggetto (Professor [the title by which Pirandello was known professionally], it's useless for you to take the script away. Tonight we'll improvise the play)." And after the successful première that night, Musco explained further that he and his actors were like racehorses trained to set off only if they hear the starter's gun: without the sounds of the gathering audience, without the houselights, they are unable to perform. The fact of the matter is that there was compatibility between Pirandello and Musco—a compatibility Pirandello recognized when he *wrote* plays for Musco while he only *adapted* them for Grasso.

The letter which he wrote to Martoglio in 1917 concerning Grasso's objections to *Il berretto a sonagli* bears quoting at some length. Grasso had made some observations about what appeared to him the unmanageable length and involvement of Ciampa's lines and complained about having to "stand by" while others were reciting *their* lines:

> Le osservazioni di Grasso, se possono aver qualche valore, riguardo al suo temperamento artistico, a cui senza dubbio si confanno più gli atti che le parole, mi pare che non ne abbiano nessuno, riguardo al lavoro stesso, come opera d'arte. Non mi pare affatto che ci siano lungaggini. L'azione e i discorsi degli altri personaggi son tutti necessari, come quelli del protagonista. La commedia, certamente, è scritta per Musco, e capisco che Grasso debba trovarsi a disagio in una parte che invece calza a pennello al Musco. Io l'ho già detto che *non sento* affatto il Grasso: il suo temperamento non m'ispira, è per me troppo primitivo e bestiale; mentre la mia arte è riflessiva. Non potrei perciò adattarmi a scrivere per lui, né adattare la mia commedia alle esigenze del suo temperamento. È inutile dunque che mi rimandi il copione. Se vuol farla, la commedia è così e resterà così. Potrei soltanto far quei tagli o, se mai, quelle modifiche, che tu alle prove con Musco stimassi necessarie e per le quali ti ho dato ampia autorizzazione. Queste sì, perché risulterebbero come volute dall'opera d'arte stessa messa alla prova della sua propria vita; mentre le modifiche e i tagli che vorrebbe il Grasso, sarebbero imposti, non dall'opera d'arte, ma dal suo speciale temperamento, ch'io stimo antitetico alla mia concezione artistica. Per Grasso starà benissimo "La morsa" che ti manderò tra giorni.

(While Grasso's observations may have some validity with respect to his own artistic temperament, to which actions are no doubt better suited than words, they have no validity, it seems to me, with respect to the play itself as a work of art. I don't at all think that there are passages that drag. The actions and the lines of the other characters are just as necessary as those of the protagonist. Doubtless, the play was written for Musco, and I can well understand that Grasso should feel ill at ease in a part which instead suits Musco to perfection. I've already said that I don't at all "feel" Grasso. His temperament doesn't inspire me: it is too primitive and bestial for me, while my art is reflective. Therefore I could

not adjust to writing for him, nor adapt my play to the exigencies of his temperament. So it is useless to send back the script.
If he wants to do the play, that is how it is and it will remain
so. I could only agree to those cuts or, possibly, changes that you
and Musco would think necessary when rehearsing the play and
for which I have given you full authorization. Those changes yes,
for they would be as though willed by the work itself when it is
tested by its own coming to life. But the changes and cuts that
Grasso wants would be imposed not by the work of art but by
his own special temperament, which I judge antithetical to my
artistic conception. For Grasso, *La morsa* will do very well, which
I shall send you in a few days.)

Musco, then, was the first actor with whom Pirandello could identify
(Ruggero Ruggeri and Marta Abba will be the later two), and because of
this affinity he was granted the privilege of becoming a collaborator, a
co-author, at the moment of rehearsal and performance. Years later, in 1935,
Pirandello was to write an essay on the historical development of the Italian
theatre, "Primato del teatro italiano," in which traces of his early relationship with Musco are still strongly apparent. He speaks with rare eloquence
of those *uomini de teatro* who created the *commedia dell'arte*, men who as
actors felt the pulse of the public and as *authors* had their own ambitions
and personal tastes, and who knew how to combine the different charge of
energy that came from each of these roles. It was because they were authors
not actors, says Pirandello in an inversion of what is usually thought of as
the static, "learned" roles of the *commedia*, that they were able to "*recitare
all'improvviso* (to improvise)" (but note how the Italian expression captures
the unrehearsed immediacy of the "suddenly"). And almost as though he were
speaking of his own turning from narrative to drama, he added: "La Commedia dell'arte nasce . . . da autori che s'accostano tanto al teatro, alla vita
del teatro, da divenire attori essi stessi, e cominciano con lo scrivere com-
medie subito più teatrali perchè non composte nella solitudine d'uno scrit-
tojo di letterato ma già quasi davanti al caldo fiato del pubblico. (The
commedia dell'arte comes into being . . . through authors who draw so close
to the theatre, to the life of the theatre, as to become actors themselves. And
they begin by writing plays that are at once more theatrical because they are
not composed in the solitude of a writer's study but almost in front of the
warm breath of the audience.)"

In a total about face from the position of the theatrical reformers of the
eighteenth century who denigrated the *commedia dell'arte*, Pirandello has

here given new dignity to the actor; the actor who is able to improvise is an author, that is, a creative artist, and not an "illustratore necessario (necessary illustrator)" as he had called him in the 1908 essay, "Illustratori, attori e traduttori," or a "traduttore" as he dubbed him without more ado in "Teatro in dialetto?" Musco, of course, as we have seen, was both actor and author. And Pirandello himself, though not technically an actor, certainly became a consummate *uomo di teatro,* one whose extraordinary interpretational gifts were remarked upon by all those fortunate enough to have been present at his reading of his plays or at rehearsals.

In addition to *Pensaci, Giacomino!,* Pirandello wrote *Liolà* (1916), *'A birritta cu' i ciancianeddi* (1916, *Il berretto a sonagli*), and *'A giarra* (1917, *La giara*) for Musco. He also translated his *La morsa, La patente* (1918), and *Tutto per bene* (1920, *Ccu' i 'nguanti gialli*) into Sicilian, but the premières of these plays were not performed by Musco, although they later (with the exception of *La morsa?*) entered his repertoire. We have already mentioned the two Sicilian plays Pirandello wrote for Martoglio. For Martoglio's Compagnia del Teatro Mediterraneo he translated Euripides' *Cyclops* (1919), and he also translated Ercole Luigi Morselli's *Glauco,* a mythological tragedy in verse, which was however never performed in translation. All in all, a quite respectable *œuvre* which would have earned him a not insignificant place in the history of the Sicilian dialect theatre had it not been overshadowed by his work in Italian and had the post–World War I years not seen the progressive dissolution of the dialect companies. Limitations of space preclude our discussing the works that exist only in dialect and those written in collaboration. The one-act plays (*La morsa, Lumíe di Sicilia, Il dovere del medico, La giara,* and *La patente*) would deserve their share of attention, but we shall have to be satisfied with referring to them in passing.

Pensaci, Giacomino!, Liolà, and *Il berretto a sonagli* are Pirandello's major Sicilian plays. Their protagonists, the mild-mannered but intransigent Professor Toti, the exuberant Liolà, and the hard pressed Ciampa, bear witness to Musco's versatility as an actor and to his liberating rather than constricting force on Pirandello. Pirandello more than once inveighed against the contemporary habit of writing plays with this or that actor already in mind. In "L'azione parlata" (1899) he criticized dramatists who permitted the virtuosities of actors to influence them. In "Illustratori, attori e traduttori" he repeated the criticism almost verbatim, adding that works that come into being under these circumstances are "opere schiave e non d'arte; perchè l'arte ha bisogno imprescindibile della sua libertà (enslaved works, not works of art, for art has an indispensable need of its liberty)." In "Teatro in dialetto?" he compares the dramatist who is asked to keep the peculiarities of his interpreters present while composing a play to a poet forced to compose a sonnet with a pre-set rhyme scheme: "Non lo scrittore deve adattarsi alle qualità dell'esecutore; ma questi a quelle dello scrittore, o meglio, dell'opera a cui deve dar vita sulla scena. (It is not the writer who must conform to the qualities of the performer, but the latter must adapt himself to the former, or better still, to the work to which he must give life on stage)." Obviously Pirandello's own relationship to Musco did not fall into the category he was criticizing.

Liolà, set in the countryside near Agrigento, is geographically the most precisely located of Pirandello's Sicilian plays. Related to this exceptional precision in setting ("campagna agrigentina") is Pirandello's choice of the particular dialect in which it was written. Not the generalized Sicilian of the contemporary regional theatre (a parallel to the "Sicilia d'importazione" which shocked him in the plays performed by Grasso and Aguglia)—"quell'ibrido linguaggio, tra il dialetto e la lingua, che è il così detto *dialetto borghese* (that hybrid language, something between dialect and Italian, that is spoken by the middle class)," as he wrote in the preface to the 1917 bilingual edition of *Liolà*—but the "pure," "sweet," "sound-rich" idiom of the peasants of the countryside of Agrigento. This was not only his native language, his mother tongue, but also the language to which he had devoted his doctoral dissertation in Romance Philology at the University of Bonn. Like all radical innovations this one too was hardly appreciated. The fact that *Liolà* was written in an authentic dialect—that its characters came into being speaking not an artificial language, be it literary Italian or *dialetto borghese,* but their *own* language—resulted in only a half-hearted success at the première. Most of the audience sat uncomprehending and only a few responded with laughter. As a matter of fact, it took many years before *Liolà* finally found its place among Pirandello's masterpieces. When it was first given in Italian, its subject matter was judged offensive. The healthy joyousness of the play—a quality Pirandello recognized while he was working on it and described to his son as "così gioconda che non pare opera mia (so happy that it doesn't seem a work of mine)"—was accepted only later when a new image of Sicily displaced the exclusive accent on the Sicily of *verismo.* The Sicily of *Liolà,* Lucio Lugnani wrote recently, is a Sicily without sulphur fumes, without *carusi,* without hunger, without villages emptied by emigration, a Sicily that does not know suspicion and jealousy, a land in which "the figures of dreams, of fairy-tales, of ancient comedy move dancing."

The plot of *Liolà* is based on an episode of *Il fu Mattia Pascal.* Liolà, a lighthearted village Don Giovanni, is already the father of three illegitimate children, whose care is entrusted to his mother, while he earns his living as "garzone, giornante; mieto, poto, falcio fieno; fo di tutto e non mi confondo mai (farmboy, day-labourer; I reap, prune hedges, gather hay; do a bit of everything and can take anything in my stride)." (The doubling and tripling here is the stylistic equivalent of Liolà's irrepressible optimism.) The play opens at harvest time as zia Croce is overseeing the work being done for her wealthy cousin, old zio Simone, whose desire for a child to whom to leave his *roba* makes him as vulnerable to trickery and fraud as messer Nicia is in *La mandragola* (a play often compared to *Liolà*). Tuzza, zia Croce's daughter, is Liolà's latest conquest, and she is pregnant. Rather than marry Liolà, however, she plots with her mother to pass her child off as zio Simone's and thus ensure that the latter's wealth will stay in the family. The victim of this scheme will be zio Simone's wife, the gentle, childless Mita. But just as in *La mandragola* the young Callimaco shows the virtuous Lucrezia how to turn her husband's foolishness to her advantage, so Liolà—in the play's wonderful act 2—convinces Mita that if she wants justice done she will have to help herself: like Tuzza, she, too, will have to have a child for zio Simone. Things now happen according to plan: through Liolà's agency there will be an apparently legitimate child to take the place of the illegitimate one in zio Simone's household, while Tuzza's child will become the fourth of Liolà's happy *cardellini* (goldfinches), his term of endearment for his brood of illegitimate children.

The parallel episode in *Il fu Mattia Pascal* is told in chapter 4, "Fu così (this is hot it happened)" (that Mattia was eventually forced to leave home). It precedes immediately the exordium of chapter 5, "La strega non si sapeva dar pace." We shall recount the episode in some detail because Pirandello's allusive and discontinuous narrative manner—so similar in technique and in effect to Verga's in *I malavoglia*—leaves many readers confused, and because a comparison between episode and play will help to define more clearly the exceptional aspects of *Liolà* in the Pirandello corpus.

Mattia, whose father had died when his sons were infants, leaving them in the care of their loving but ineffectual mother, is enjoying a free and easy existence while Batta Malagna, who is supposed to look after the brothers' property, is blithely digging away at it. "La talpa! la talpa! (the mole, the mole!)" Mattia's strong-minded aunt exclaims whenever she thinks of him. Like zio Simone before the opening of the play, Batta Malagna had long been married to a woman who bore him no children. Upon her death he marries again, reluctantly but determined to have an heir to whom to leave his ill-gotten wealth. (Zio Simone is stingy but Batta Malagna, in a darkening of the vision, is downright dishonest.) He chooses Oliva, a young, healthy, attractive girl, as virtuous as Mita, whom Mattia himself (like Liolà, Mita)

had been courting. Malagna and Oliva do not have a child, and Malagna
begins to mistreat her. So far, novel and play follow an almost identical narrative line. But in the novel a second action is developing which will intersect
the first. Mattia's best friend, Pomino (there is no counterpart for this
character in *Liolà*, Liolà and zio Simone—except for Liolà's three small sons—
being the only male characters in its *dramatis personae*), becomes interested
in a girl who is the daughter of a cousin of Malagna and discovers that mother
and daughter—the *vedova* Pescatore (= zia Croce) and Romilda (= Tuzza)—
are trying to entice the old man into an illicit relationship with Romilda.
To protect Oliva and to back up Pomino's suit, Mattia intervenes. But
Romilda, instead of falling in love with Pomino, falls in love with Mattia,
and their "game" is turned into an affair. Like Liolà, Mattia is ready to marry
the girl he has seduced, and like Liolà, he is rejected because mother and
daughter have more profitable plans. What follows in novel and play is identical: Malagna, who is expecting to be made a father by Romilda, discovers
that Oliva is pregnant as well. Aware that he has been duped and by whom,
and moreover being in a position of power over Mattia (something zio Simone
is not over Liolà), Malagna forces him to marry Romilda. The family that
thus comes into being is doomed to dissension and unhappiness for the *vedova*
Pescatore, now mother-in-law ("strega," *par excellence*), will never be able
to forgive Mattia his status of impecunious son-in-law.

Because of the customary compartmentalization imposed on Pirandello's
works by critics, the relationship between the *Il fu Mattia Pascal* episode and
its reworking in *Liolà* has received only scanty, superficial attention. The
most striking contrasts have been remarked: that *Liolà* is set in Sicily while
Il fu Mattia Pascal begins in Liguria, that Liolà is a peasant while Mattia
is a bourgeois, that the play is "homogeneous" while the narrative episode
is weighed down by moralizing and "humorizing" (Gramsci). As far back
as 1927 Ferdinando Pasini pointed out that *Il fu Mattia Pascal* is only a par-
tial source for *Liolà:* the character of the protagonist, and indeed his name,
deriving from the 1904 story "La mosca": "Lavorare e cantare, tutto a regola
d'arte. Non per nulla lo chiamavano Liolà, il poeta. (To work and to sing,
both done to perfection. It was with good reason that they called him Liolà,
the poet.)" The fact of the matter is that Liolà has a buoyancy which the
"darker vision" of *Il fu Mattia Pascal* precludes. There is something auroral,
something of "the rich unfolding morn," in *Liolà,* completely lacking in the
troubled world of *Il fu Mattia Pascal:* we could imagine Liolà gaily dancing
with his shadow; Mattia is overcome with pity at the sight of his. Mattia
belongs to the family of the anti-heroes, the "inetti" (inept) of Italian naturalist
and realist fiction from Svevo's *Una vita* to Moravia's *Gli indifferenti*. He

cannot, or he can no longer, cope with the difficulties of life except to retreat before them: the first time he runs away from home; the second time he accepts the personality that circumstances have created for him and becomes that paradox, the still-living late Mattia Pascal. Where Mattia is inept, a failure even insofar as the world of work is concerned, Liolà is wonderfully successful. Involved in the same intrigue (as far as the episode we have been considering is concerned), motivated by similar drives and emotions, the one eludes the trap while the other is permanently caught in it. The sun of Sicily, the songs and dances, the music and choreography with which some spectacular modern performances (such as the one at the Temple of Segesta in 1968) have enriched this fundamentally straightforward traditional play, can thus be considered "objective correlatives" of that most exhilarating of feelings, the feeling of having miraculously escaped.

In *Il berretto a sonagli* Ciampa's "escape" is won at a different price and finds him not singing at the end but giving vent to his feelings (not unlike papà Camillo in *Capannetta*) in "un'orribile risata, di rabbia, di selvaggio piacere e di disprezzo a un tempo (a horrible burst of laughter, rage, savage pleasure, and despair all at once)." The play takes place not in the out-of-doors, in the revived land of Theocritus and the pastoral, but in the claustrophobic milieu of an over-furnished parlour in that typical "cittadina dell'interno della Sicilia" so harshly described by Signora Ignazia's lines in *Questa sera si recita a soggetto.*

The first scene brings together the female characters of the play. In a paroxysm of her habitual jealousy, Signora Beatrice Fioríca is determined to find out about her husband's suspected infidelity and expose it to public view. Fana, her old servant, counsels age-old wisdom and a measure of resignation. But the junk-dealer La Saracena (a witch figure similar to the *vedova* Pescatore in *Il fu Mattia Pascal* and Madama Pace in *Sei personaggi*) supports Beatrice in her rebellion against her husband, and has come with a supposedly fool-proof plan for catching Fioríca and his reputed mistress *in flagrante.* The scene, like Pirandello's *exordia* in general, is characterized by the scintillating rapidity of the dialogue: the exposition of the situation takes place within the discussion of that *topos* of folklore and literature, "What should a wife's attitude be towards an errant husband?" Beatrice's feelings have all the earmarks of those of a woman bent on "liberating" herself and establishing her rights: "Mi libero! mi libero! mi libero!" is her thrice repeated cry in answer tò Fana's cautious warning that she is ruining herself. Pirandello's own judgment of Beatrice, besides being implicit in the outcome of the play, is already stated in the stage direction at her first appearance: "sui trent'anni, pallida, isterica, tutta furie e abbattimenti subitanei (about

thirty, pale, hysterical, all sudden fits of activity and depression)." Hysteria
in its quasi-medical acceptance, it should be remembered, is a distinguishing
feature of almost all his sterile women protagonists, and always of the fragile,
self-centred, disruptive ones, such as Beatrice in this case or Silia Gala in
Il giuoco delle parti (but *not* of Livia in *La ragione degli altri,* to whom the
first part but not the second part of the characterization would apply).

Of the three women in scene 1 only Fana has thought of the possible
consequence of Beatrice's determination for Ciampa, signor Fiorìca's clerk
and husband of his supposed mistress. Only she, like Liolà with respect to
Mita, and Mattia with respect to Oliva, has thought of him as a human being
rather than as a stumbling block to be temporarily removed. It is the presence
of Ciampa—that is, the presence of a fourth involved individual—which turns
the situation in *Il berretto a sonagli* from the pattern of the conventional
triangle (such as in *La morsa* or *La ragione degli altri*), with its accent on
the psychological complications of the private emotion of love, to a relationship in which the public demands of saving face—or of "honour," to remain
within the terminology of the Sicilian milieu in which the action takes place—
play a preponderant role. In this respect *Il berretto a sonagli* belongs with
Il dovere del medico and *'A vilanza* (the play in which the theme of the two
couples is developed most directly) rather than with the two plays just mentioned. Ciampa's position as signor Fiorìca's subordiante is an added complication and has led some critics to emphasize the sociological aspects of
the play. Luigi Ferrante, for instance, feels that Ciampa's "rebellion," his desire
for social respectability, reaches beyond the circumstances of his wife's
presumed infidelity and rests on the "ancient humiliation . . . of the 'poor,
old' servant vis-à-vis his 'rich, young and handsome' master"—an insight
somewhat weakened by Ferrante's incomplete citing of self not as *povero
e vecchio* but as *brutto, vecchio, povero,* reversing the order of the adjec-
tives he uses to describe his master, *ricco, giovane, bello.* On the meaning
of that reversal—to which rhetoric and not just ideology might have contributed—the last word does not seem to have been spoken.

Be that as it may, a sociological reading of *Il berretto a sonagli,* especially if pushed to extremes, results in diminishing what Pirandello surely considered Ciampa's dominant characterization, his existential suffering. Ciampa
has two entrances in the play. When he first comes on stage in act 1 he already
bears the marks of Pirandello's typically "disturbed" protagonist: his thick,
long hair is dishevelled; he has a madman's eyes that "lampeggiano duri, acuti,
mobilissimi dietro i grossi occhiali a staffa (flash hard, sharp, unsteadily
behind his thick spectacles)." When he reappears in act 2, after La Saracena's
plan has been implemented, the ravages of suffering have increased: "Ciam-

pa entra per la comune, cadaverico, con l'abito e la faccia imbrattati di terra; la fronte ferita; il colletto sbottonato; la cravatta sciolta, e gli occhiali in mano. (Ciampa enters by the stage door. He is deathly pale. His suit and face are soiled with earth, his forehead wounded, his collar unbuttoned, his tie loose. He is carrying his glasses in his hand.)"

The change that has occurred in Ciampa, his virtual destruction and its outward signs, is analogous to the change Chiàrchiaro undergoes in *La patente* (he has only one entrance but the spectator knows in what way the "new" man differs from the old); the change "Enrico IV" suffers (not only through the fall from his horse but later, too, in the course of the action on stage); the change in Sampognetta in *Questa sera si recita a soggetto* (between his initial appearance as *Il vecchio attore brillante* and his death as Signora Ignazia's husband). In each case something irreparable has taken place, something that has torn the mask of convention from the face of an individual who had from the beginning been conceived as in some respects "exceptional": Chiàrchiaro because of his reputation as *jettatore* (bearer of the evil eye), "Enrico IV" because of his "strangeness" which sets him apart from the other young men in Matilda's entourage, Sampognetta (the least "exceptional") because "distratto, fischia sempre (absent-minded, he is always whistling)." Ciampa's atypicalness, which by itself would show that he is no "representative" of his class, is that, like Dr Fileno and Anselmo Paleari, he is the inventor of a theory.

The theory is that of the three-keyed "instrument" that regulates men's actions in their relations with one another:

> . . . abbiamo tutti come tre corde d'orologio in testa. La *seria*, la *civile*, la *pazza*. Sopra-tutto, dovendo vivere in società, ci serve la civile; per cui sta qua, in mezzo alla fronte. . . . Ma può venire il momento che le acque s'intorbidano. E allora . . . allora io cerco, prima, di girare qua la corda seria, per chiarire, rimettere le cose a posto, dare le mie ragioni, dire quattro e quattr'otto, senza tante storie, quello che devo. Che se poi non mi riesce in nessun modo, sferro, signora, la corda pazza, perdo la vista degli occhi e non so più quello che faccio!

> (We all have something like three keys in our heads. The *thinking* key, the *civil* key, and the *crazy* key. Since we have to live among our fellow-men, we need the civil key above all. That is why it's here, in the middle of the forehead. . . . But a moment may come when the waters get muddy. And then . . . then I try

first of all to turn the thinking key, to clear things up, get them
straightened out, state my point of view, say what I have to say
without beating about the bush. But, if I can't manage it somehow,
if things get too difficult, why then I turn the crazy key like mad,
lose the light of reason, and no longer know what I'm doing!)

Compared to *lanterninosofia* and *filosofia del lontano* Ciampa's
"remedy" deals in more immediate fashion with problems of everyday life.
Where *lanterninosofia* attempts to explain the waxing and waning of beliefs
on a large cultural scale and *filosofia del lontano* suggests a way whereby
anguish can be minimized, the theory of the three-keyed instrument
generalizes the basic observation that behaviour in public and behaviour in
private are not necessarily the same, that individuals carry around with them
their *personae*. In what Fifí, Beatrice's brother, perceives as a most amusing
retelling of the essence of the relationship between his sister and her husband, Ciampa describes the war waged by the *pupo-marito* and the *pupa-
moglie* (husband-turned-puppet and wife-turned-puppet) and its temporary
pacification outside the privacy of the home: "Dentro, si strappano i capelli,
si vanno con le dita negli occhi; appena fuori però, si mettono a braccetto:
corda civile lei, *corda civile* lui, *corda civile* tutto il pubblico che, come vi
vede passare, chi si scosta di qua, chi si scosta di là, sorrisi, scappellate,
riverenze—e i due pupi godono, tronfi d'orgoglio e di soddisfazione! (Inside,
they pull each other's hair, they stick their fingers in each other's eyes; but
as soon as they are outside, they walk arm in arm. She turns her *civil key*,
he turns his, and everyone else does the same. And those that see you passing by—some step aside this way, some that way, they smile, doff their hats,
bow—and the two *pupi* rejoice, puffed up with pride and satisfaction!)"
Indeed, the whole of *Il berretto a sonagli* could be seen as an illustration of
the three-keys theory, a demonstration of the correctness of Ciampa's insight
and of the "model" he has constructed. When, after having tried reasoning
and persuasion, Ciampa "turns the crazy key like mad," so hard that he "hyp-
notizes" Beatrice into giving proof that she is insane so that her accusations
may appear to have been caused not by facts but by the imaginings of an
unbalanced mind, he has on his side the approval of her family and even
of the head of police, Spanò. All these people, the chorus of the socially well-
adjusted, are convinced that Ciampa's is the only possible way for restoring
the order upset by Beatrice's excess.

But in spite of the conclusion which in the spirit of comedy celebrates
accommodation, the ending of *Il berretto a sonagli* is not a happy but a bitter
one. Like "Enrico IV"'s, Ciampa's bitterness is corrosive. How he would

love to play the madman: "Fare il pazzo! Potessi farlo io, come piacerebbe
a me! Sferrare, signora, qua *indica la tempia sinistra col solito gesto* per dav-
vero tutta la corda pazza, cacciarmi fino agli orecchi il berretto a sonagli
della pazzia e scendere in piazza a sputare in faccia alla gente la verità. (To
play the madman! If I could do it, as I'd like to do it! To wind here *he points
to the left side of his forehead with the usual gesture* the whole key of insanity,
to pull down the fool's cap of the madman to my ears, and get out into the
streets to spit out the truth into people's faces.)"

Surely it is not without significance that whereas it was possible to discuss
Liolà without using quotations, in the case of *Il berretto a sonagli* Pirandello's
language, whether in the descriptive passages (the stage directions) or in
Ciampa's lines, imposes itself to the point of forcing us to repeat it. This
is because the play rests so heavily, so exclusively, on its protagonist. Even
more than the other plays written for Musco, *Il berretto a sonagli* shows
the impact of that "star" (*grande attore*) on the author. It is no doubt its
bigger-than-life protagonist, condemned to live amid the hollow men and
women that surround him, that accounts for a certain lack of balance in the
play. The situation of an "exceptional" individual hounded by the petty persons around him is of course not unique to *Il berretto a sonagli,* and indeed,
in comparison to signor Ponza and signora Frola in *Così è (se vi pare)* or
to the mad emperor in *Enrico IV,* Ciampa is not so much hounded as
overlooked. But in these other plays a richer cast of characters and a more
complicated and varied stage business fill in the gap left by the absence of
an antagonist commensurate to the protagonist. In *Il berretto a sonagli* the
scenes in which Ciampa does not appear are slight, much slighter, for instance, than the scenes in *La patente* where Chiàrchiaro is not on stage, for
Judge D'Andrea is after all in his way an equal to the distraught, hate-filled,
self-appointed *jettatore.* The exceptional importance of the protagonist sets
Il berretto a sonagli apart among the corpus of Pirandello's Sicilian plays,
a fact underlined by its having had to wait until 1936 for another great dialect
actor, Eduardo De Filippo, for performances comparable to those of Musco.

Agostino Toti in *Pensaci, Giacomino!* would by age, position, and
manner hardly appear a likely candidate for the role of protagonist and
subverter of accepted values. Pirandello describes him as he first emerges from
the natural science laboratory in the secondary school where he is teaching
as a *vecchietto* of over seventy, not too steady on his legs, wearing cloth shoes,
a skull cap, and a long green muffler around his neck with the ends dangling
down his chest and back. From the room behind him surges the din of a
class in uproar: Professor Toti is incapable of keeping discipline because he
understands *la ragione degli altri,* in this case the healthy animal spirits of

insubordination of his young charges. The principal of the school would like
to see him retire, but he is too poor and too lonely to do so. Moreover, though
he does not have a theory like Ciampa or Dr Fileno, he has a plan: he hopes
to get married. Like don Diego Alcozèr in *Il turno,* another spry septuagenar-
ian, he looks forward to spending the remaining years of his life in the company of a cheerful young wife. But there is also a measure of rancour in Toti—
missing in don Alcozèr who has had no financial worries. Toti wants to
get his revenge for having been an underpaid civil servant all his life: by marrying a young wife he will presumably be forcing the government to pay her
many years of pension as his widow. "Ma sa che lei è un bel tomo, professore?
Mi congratulo! Uomo di spirito! (Do you realize that you're quite a character,
my dear professor? Congratulations! You're a man of ingenuity!)," the principal comments, recognizing Toti's "exceptionalness," when he hears all this.

But as is usual in Pirandello's fictional universe, Toti encounters difficulties in trying to bend circumstances to his will. First of all, the girl he
has chosen to be his wife, the school janitor's teenage daughter, already has
a lover (Giacomino) and is pregnant. Surprised but undaunted, Toti manages
to fit this development into his plan: it simply means that what he had expected to happen later has already happened. He had never thought that he'd
be anything but a "father" to Lillina and a "grandfather" to her children
anyway. The second difficulty stems from the inability of the literal-minded
people who surround Toti to make that distinction between self and role
he is so eminently capable of making. "Altro è la professione, altro è l'uomo
(The profession is one thing, the man another)" is his explicit statement to
the principal on this point during the very first scene of the play. But while
Toti is "quite a character," the others are quite conventional. Thus, instead
of being grateful for the solution that marriage offers for their daughter's
predicament, Cinquemani and his wife would prefer to safeguard her reputation (and incidentally punish her) in the usual way by keeping the birth of
the child a secret. And later when Toti uses his unexpected inheritance to
strengthen the relationship between Giacomino and Lillina, they can think
only of the wrong done *them* when Giacomino—and not they—is put in
charge of Lillina's financial interests.

The most serious, indeed the only real threat to Toti's plans for Lillina
comes from Giacomino's bigoted older sister, Rosaria, and from Padre Landolina, her spiritual guide. When Toti recognizes the threat, he acts as Liolà
does in defence of the innocent Mita. He acts not to defend his own small
claim to comfort and happiness in old age, but to defend the rights of the
wife and mother of the *de facto,* though not *de jure,* family that already
exists. In the magnificently eloquent final scene Toti tracks his enemy to her

home and in the "salottino quasi monacale (almost monastic parlour)" of *casa* Delisi convinces Giacomino that he is committed for life and that he could find no better wife than Lillina. "Non posso piú sciogliermi, Rosaria (I can no longer free myself, Rosaria)," Giacomino tells his sister in the *dénouement* of the action. The story thus ends happily with a "marriage," as is suitable in the world of comedy. The *play,* however, ends differently. Like *La patente, Cosí è (se vi pare)*, and *Sei personnaggi*, it has a spectacular finale that follows the *dénouement.* Immediately after Giacomino's declaration just quoted, this finale sounds an anti-clerical note daring and total that one may speculate that only bravura acting and the dialect incomprehensible to the majority of the audience in which the play was originally performed saved it from censorship. Using Christ's famous admonition to Satan, *Vade, retro!,* Toti bars the way to Padre Landolina as Giacomino and his small son cross the threshold and escape from the self-appointed guardians of public morality. Like Chiàrchiaro's apparently excessive reaction to the death of Judge D'Andrea's bird in *La patente,* Toti's violent outburst at the end—after so much diplomacy and forethought—points back to the tremendous pressure to which he has been subjected but which he has successfully withstood. Like Liolà and unlike Chiàrchiaro and Ciampa, Toti is a winner. But the nature-alienated milieu in which his victory takes place robs it of the joyousness that is *Liolà's.*

Pirandello's Sicilian fictions reflect a social and psychological environment perhaps most inclusively characterized by Nicola Ciarletta, who has probably written the best essay on Pirandello's *Sicilianità,* when he speaks of the "incredible difficulties" of life in it. The economic difficulties are probably the more familiar and more accessible to the reader. Where Pirandello's work includes them it is closest to Verga's and also offers a possibility for flight from disturbing and painful pessimism through the dream of a Utopia to come. But it is the psychological difficulties that are the more significant for Pirandello. Here again Ciarletta provides a striking formulation: he describes the actions of "Enrico IV" as "a poor man's revenge," the revenge of "someone who is accustomed to hiding himself," that is, accustomed to trying to protect his privacy and dignity in the face of poverty and want. The attitude, exemplified in Ciampa and Chiàrchiaro for instance, may be difficult to understand and sympathize with in the age of expanding welfare states, but it underlines the actions of many of Pirandello's most important characters. To such an individual, to what we might call the wounded man, it is almost impossible, as Judge D'Andrea has understood, "to do good." The "poor man," everyman (as can be seen in the case of the wealthy and socially protected "Enrico IV," which enlarges the meaning of poverty), ends

up by seeing in every other man a potential rival, an enemy. Where there
is no sense of community, men remain isolated, "each an island to himself,"
as Pirandello wrote in the speech on Verga.

Secrecy, reticence, guarded statements, tortuous reasoning, scepticism,
the camouflage of irony and paradox, the cultivation of eccentricity become
so many strategies of self-protection. The mask almost becomes the face,
the role the man. The margin of freedom that can be won is minimal: the
setting up of an ingenious argument (Liolà's in convincing Mita that she must
become "dishonest" in order to gain back her position of respected wife,
Ciampa's in showing Beatrice's family that she must go "mad" in order to
undo the harm she had done by "being right"); the bending of another's will
to one's own (zi' Dima's victory over Don Lolò in *La giara,* Toti's defeat of
"public opinion" in *Pensaci, Giacomino!*); retreat before a *fait accompli* that
can no longer be undone (Micuccio's rejection of Sina in *Lumíe di Sicilia*).
The "poor man's revenge" elicits pity and consternation from reader and spectator. Pity is the emotion more easily dealt with: it is both evoked and
neutralized by the distance that separates fictional from real life. Consternation is a different matter: it obliterates and denies distance. We are horrified
by an action that we recognize as belonging potentially to our own world—
and it is such actions that conclude many of Pirandello's plays.

Repression and explosiveness, in Giudice's formulation, are the distinguishing features of the Sicilian personality. At one end a static, rigid
society; at the other the one mad moment that will spell permanent disaster.
In Pirandello's fictions the solution to a personal predicament can never be
simply to walk away from the situation, to start afresh somewhere else.
Ciampa feels a different man when he is sent to Palermo on an errand—
"Appena cammino per le strade di una grande città, già non mi pare piú di
camminare sulla terra: m'imparadiso! (As soon as I walk through the streets
of a large city, I no longer feel I'm treading the earth: I'm filled with paradise!)"—but he must come back to the "cittadina dell'interno della Sicilia"
which is his prison. Mattia Pascal gets away from the *vedova* Pescatore but
his bid for self-fulfilment fails and the only freedom he can find at the end
is to write the story of his life. Marta Ajala sets off to become independent,
to make a life for herself in which she will be person not object, but at the
end she is back with the husband who had driven her out. In *L'aria del continente* (not claimed by Pirandello as his work but not repudiated either) the
genius loci dogs that protagonist's steps to the point of re-establishing for him
the typical situation of the *cornuto* (cuckold) with respect to the unpreju-
diced "continental" mistress he had picked up in Rome and who turns out
to be instead just another Sicilian. Whatever movement, whatever variegated

life there is in Pirandello's world, the situations his characters find themselves in must be solved *in situ,* at the still centre of the storm. But the solution of a situation (the *dénouement* in a play) is not necessarily the resolution of the psychological difficulties that have brought it about. As a matter of fact, for the difficulties that lie at the heart of Pirandello's world view there can be no conclusive solutions. There can be no remedies, for such remedies would spell their disappearance and dissolve the tensions that kept the world he knew alive and generated the energy which made it possible for him to give it artistic form. The beginnings of Pirandello's activity as a dramatist are inextricably involved with his meeting with Musco, the "concretization" as it were of the very tensions that demanded to be expressed. It is significant that this "concretization" took place in the figure of an individual for this shows how rock-firm Pirandello was in his attachment to the geocentric universe from whose centre man—Western man—in spite of the Copernican revolution had not yet been displaced.

MAURICE VALENCY

Pirandello: A New Conception of Theatre

The new drama came but slowly to Italy. In the pre-war period, before 1914, the Italian stage was dominated by star-actors and actresses who toured the Italian cities with their own companies each season with a new repertory of plays. There were few resident companies. The great luminaries— Tommaso Salvini, Eleanora Duse, Irma and Emma Grammatica, Ruggero Ruggeri—were accustomed to think of plays mainly as vehicles for the display of their talents, and everything written for the stage was subject to summary revision to that end. In the pre-war years D'Annunzio was the reigning Italian dramatist, and the theatre was under strong romantic influence. The first productions of Ibsen's plays aroused wrath, and then wonder. Shaw's plays were discussed by the learned, but they aroused little popular interest. Chekhov was found puzzling. Henri Becque excited attention: *La Parisienne* shocked its audiences into some awareness of French realism, and the Italian managers soon saw the commercial possibilities of Donnay, Porto-Riche, Curel, and Vildrac, the heirs and next of kin of the Théâtre-libre.

Pirandello had come to Rome in the hope of making a career as a dramatist. In 1896 he finished a play in three acts called *Il nibbio* (*The Hawk*) but after an unpleasant experience with Flavio Andò, the actor to whom he submitted it, he developed a studied contempt for the stage, and henceforth professed to know nothing about Italian drama from the time of Goldoni. Nevertheless, in 1899 he wrote a piece for the *Marzocco* of Florence in which he expressed very decided views regarding the composition of plays:

> In our day most dramatic works are essentially narrative, draw-
> ing for their subject-matter upon novels or *novelle*. This can only

be a mistake: first, because in general a narrative is not easily reducible to the proportions of the stage; second, because these proportions are further narrowed and shrunken by the excessive and (in my opinion) misapplied rigidity of modern stage technique.

Pirandello was at this time thirty-two, and he was beginning to be known in journalistic circles as a writer of some originality, but chiefly as a writer of short stories. His compatriot Luigi Capuana had long ago persuaded him to turn from poetry to fiction, and in 1894 he had published a novel, *L'esclusa,* in realistic style. It excited little interest. That same year he began to submit *novelle* to the newspapers. His first volume of collected stories, *Amori senza amore* (1894), clearly demonstrated his talent, and in the following years he devoted his efforts almost exclusively to the production of short narrative pieces.

As a writer of *novelle* he was amazingly prolific. From 1903 to 1920, volume succeeded volume in a seemingly inexhaustible stream of narrative. His best stories are leisurely monologues spoken by a narrator in the company of an imaginary listener whose reactions are casually noted by the speaker so that both narrator and listener are characterized dramatically in the course of the tale. The narrator is invariably a man of tact, warm, excitable, informed, and at the same time curiously diffident, a gentleman who is careful not to presume on the fleeting intimacy of an occasion which brings two strangers together long enough to exchange a confidence. The listener is never impatient. He is a sensitive and sympathetic character who never obtrudes a remark, but whose occasional smile or nod of understanding is immediately reflected in the narrator's speech. In this manner each short story becomes a little play within which the anecdote is developed between a pair of actors, one of whom is the author and the other the audience.

Such stories as "Acqua amara" and "Ciàula scopre la luna"—poignant tales told with a smile—are in the highest sense dramatic; but the type of story which Pirandello tells better than anyone is intimate in a way that cannot be reproduced under the conditions of the theatre. In the theatre there are too many people for this sort of intimacy. Indeed when Pirandello visualized his stories in terms of the living actor he lost, inevitably, much of his grace as a raconteur. In his day the Italian dramatist was by temper and training never so far removed from the operatic tradition as to transcend wholly the melodramatic tendencies of the profession; and if, by some miracle, he managed this feat, the actor did not. Doubtless in his early article in the *Marzocco* Pirandello had such difficulties in mind, and his observations with regard to the adaptation of stories for the stage were both wise and just.

Unfortunately when he came to write for the theatre thirteen years later he did not heed them. His first ventures in the drama at that time were straightforward adaptations of his own *novelle,* and of the forty-three plays he wrote during his long career in the theatre, by far the greater part were drawn from stories he had written long before. His two masterpieces, however, were written directly for the stage, and in both cases he broke new ground in the theatre.

In 1893 he had written of Ibsen:

> It is enough for someone to be momentarily incomprehensible for him to be immediately surrounded by a swarm of admiring individuals as insistent and oppressive, if I may be allowed a vulgar image, as flies buzzing about a gob of spit.

At this time, also, he appeared to have no affinity with the Symbolists in France. He was a Realist. He did not understand Mallarmé. He disliked Verlaine; and in 1896 he expressed a strong distaste for the irrationalism of Maurice Barrès and those of his circle. But, as with most writers of his time, his views were liable to change without notice. Twenty-five years later he himself was making a virtue of incomprehensibility; the same swarm of admiring individuals who had earned his contempt in the early days was now buzzing merrily about him, and his work was so far advanced along Symbolist lines that Marinetti claimed him as a Futurist.

"With the help of God," he wrote in December 1909, "I will never write plays . . . to me a play is an illustration in a book, or a translation beside the original; it either spoils or diminishes what it represents." His immediate circle of friends, however, included a number of playwrights, theatre directors, and drama critics, among them Giustino Ferri, Ugo Fleres, Lucio d'Ambra, and Nino Martoglio. For a long time Pirandello refused to participate in their discussions of the theatre. It is said that when their talk turned in that direction he at once withdrew into a game of solitaire. But in 1912 Martoglio persuaded him to adapt one of his *novelle,* "La morsa" ("The Vise") for the Sicilian stage in Rome. The play did well. Other adaptations followed. They were all written in dialect for the Sicilian theatre, and all dealt with Sicilian subjects.

The Italian theatre meanwhile was undergoing a striking transformation. A new school of playwrights was making its mark, and a new type of realism was being very rapidly developed. Luigi Chiarelli's *La maschera e il volto* (*The Mask and the Face*) was presented for the first time on 31 May 1916, at the Teatro Argentina in Rome. It created a sensation. The author called his play a *grottesco*. The "grotesque" was a term Victor Hugo had used to describe a dramatic genre that would combine tragedy with comedy in the manner of Shakespeare. *The Mask and the Face* was neither Shakespearean nor romantic; but the term was apt, so much so that in the following years everything that was new in the Italian drama was likely to be called grotesque.

The Mask and the Face is a funny comedy with tragic overtones. The protagonist Paolo has solemnly proclaimed that his sense of personal honor is so delicate that if ever he should find his wife Savina unfaithful he would, without a moment's hesitation, kill her. Quite unexpectedly he is put to the test. But, having made his fatal discovery, he also discovers, to his astonishment, that he is not at all the man he thought he was. In spite of everything, he loves his wife, and has no wish whatever to kill her. He does, however, feel the pressure of public opinion so strongly that he pretends to act in accordance with his public image. Savina is spirited away and changes her name. Paolo then declares that she is dead and that he has cleared his name. He is duly arrested, tried, and sentenced, and on his return from prison is borne home in triumph by his fellow townsmen. But these extravagances are more than he can bear. When Savina secretly visits him, he decides to put an end to his pretense and to affirm his autonomy as a free man: "I am not going to render an account of my life to anyone, neither to society, nor my friends, nor to the law, nothing, it's enough!" But in spite of this declaration of independence it is necessary for him to fly the coop with his wife in order to escape the legal consequences of his fraud.

The play, as Tilgher pointed out, makes no comment on the situation. Paolo's psychic somersault is presented with comic gravity, simply as a fact. The fact, of course, speaks for itself, and it found immediate acceptance. Henceforth the way was open on the Italian stage for a full-scale assault on the time-honored traditions of Italian culture. What was under fire in *The Mask and the Face* was, ostensibly, the ideal. The approach to the unquestionable duty of the Italian husband to avenge his honor was in this case realistic, and from this viewpoint the result was comic. Chiarelli did not ridicule the ideal of feminine purity, nor the blood-sacrifice which had so long sustained it. The joke is at the expense of the individual who submits to a social code in which he does not really believe, and which nevertheless operates tyrannically to dictate his behavior. What is serious in the play is the tragic relation of the social group to the individuals who comprise it, and the consequent despotism of customs in which perhaps nobody any longer believes. Thus Chiarelli took up in 1916 the assault on the ideal which Ibsen had initiated with *Ghosts* in 1881. The result was a new wave of realism in the Italian theatre.

The Mask and the Face was Chiarelli's masterpiece. His later plays maintained his ironic mood, but they were not equally cogent. *La scala di seta* (*The Silken Ladder*) is an interesting study of a demagogue, but the caricature is not wholly convincing. *Chimere* is excessively melodramatic, and *La morte degli amanti* is confusing. All these plays in some way illustrate the essential theme of the grotesque, the contrast between the conventional face which society imposes on the individual and the feelings which are the spontaneous expressions of his personality—in general terms, the contrast of truth and fiction. Underlying this theme was an even more basic issue—the conflict of freedom and order.

The school of the Grotesque included a number of ambitious young dramatists, among them Luigi Antonelli, Carlo Veneziano, Enrico Cavacchioli, Fausto Martini, and Massimo Bontempelli. With the exception of Martini, none of these was highly talented as a playwright. After Chiarelli it was Piermaria Rosso di San Secondo who most ably developed this genre, and it was he who put Pirandello in touch with the new realism in the theatre.

Rosso was more directly in touch with the French theatre than Chiarelli, and he did not follow Chiarelli's line. He was an Idealist. Like Ibsen he found a source of dramatic tension in the contrast between the cold Northern temper and the Southern—"the South all impulse and passion, the North all discipline and will"—an idea traceable to Buckle's *History of Civilization*. The ideal world, Rosso believed, is common to all men in their infancy, but when Northerners grow up they believe that the phenomenal world is real, whereas the Southerner remains in this respect a child. The realities of everyday life do not convince the Southerner; consequently he spends his life wandering aimlessly "between dream and day," an alien and a transient in an unreal world. In this dubious state of mind, life seems to him in the nature of a practical joke, until the magic moment when suddenly a vision of the ideal world of his childhood flashes before his eyes and transforms the shadowy reality around him into something wonderful and true. But the moment of insight is pitifully brief, and when the intuition of eternity fades away what is left is only a cry of anguish. In Rosso's "Elegie a Maryke," in "Amara," and in "Per fare l'alba" the influence of French Symbolism is unmistakable. It requires no effort to see in Rosso's poetry the influence of Mallarmé.

In the theatre Rosso's fame rested chiefly on three plays—*Marionette! che passione!* (1918), *La bella adormentata* (1919), and *La scala* (1926). The first deals in mysterious fashion with three characters whom life destroys. Each feels himself to be a tragic figure, suffering mightily. In reality all three are no more than puppets on strings, without volition of their own. Love is the hand that works their strings. They are the toys of love, and when it is done with them, it casts them aside like toys. Their grandiose postures and their displays of passion, consequently, can only move the spectator to laughter, for what seems tragic to the figures in the guignol is merely comic to the objective observer; their tragedy is a farce. In this play Rosso made the idea of the Grotesque entirely explicit. The idea was far from new, but the style was original, and Rosso's irony made a deep, though distinctly unpleasant, impression on an audience that was attuned mainly to romantic and sentimental displays. The relation of Rosso's play to the work of Maeterlinck and the doctrine of Schopenhauer in his *Metaphysics of the Love of the Sexes* was, of course, unmistakable, but few of the contemporary critics were disposed to discuss it.

The Sleeping Beauty is another sort of play, but it shares in some ways the abstract quality of *Marionettes! What Passion!* The play is subtitled—doubtless in deference to the synaesthetic notions of the Symbolists—"una avventura colorata (a colored adventure)." La Bella is the village prostitute. She lives in a dream, entirely acquiescent. She has neither will nor any sense of guilt and is a pure manifestation of life, so simple that people marvel at its ideal quality. Quite unexpectedly she finds herself with child. At this point she renounces her profession and takes the child to the notary who first seduced her and who is thus in some sense answerable for it. The play has a *raisonneur* in the person of The Black Man of the Sulfur, a romantic character whom life has made a cynic: perhaps it is the author. Life to him is a colored adventure, and he colors it further by forcing the notary to marry La Bella in accordance with right and justice.

Rosso di San Secondo was some twenty years younger than Pirandello, and one of his closest friends. When Rosso became editor of *Il Messagero della Domenica,* we are told, Pirandello stopped by his office every afternoon. It was through Rosso that he turned from his Sicilian plays to the avant-garde drama that the Grotteschi were trying to develop. In 1918 Pirandello wrote admiringly of *Marionette! che passione!:* "Here every logical preparation, every logical support has been abolished. . . . The apparent lack of logic . . . is in fact the supreme logic." Two years later he was prepared to give a more scholarly interpretation of the Teatro del grottesco. In an article published 27 February 1920, in *L'Idea nazionale* he wrote:

> A good phrase to define the most significant modern works of
> the Grotesque is "transcendental farce." . . . Hegel has explained
> that the subject, the only sure reality, can smile at the vain appear-
> ances of the world. It constructs them, but it can also destroy
> them; it need not take its own creations seriously. Hence we have
> irony, that force which, according to Tieck, allows the poet to
> dominate his subject-matter. And, according to Friedrich Schlegel,

> it is through irony that this same subject-matter is reduced to a
> perpetual parody, a transcendental farce. . . . The farce of the
> Grotesque includes in its tragedy its parody and its caricature, not
> as extraneous superposed elements, but as its own shadow, the
> awkward shadow of every tragic gesture.

It is doubtful if either Chiarelli or Rosso intended their plans to carry this much weight, but the idea of the grotesque certainly warranted a philosophical interpretation, and its later consequences may be studied to advantage in the plays and the theories of Ionesco and Dürrenmatt, among the other specialists in transcendental farce. Pirandello's sense of reality had by this time been seriously shaken. The mutability of his fortunes and his wife's nagging delusions had done much to undermine his sense of the world's stability, and the senseless destructiveness of the war years greatly aggravated his mental discomfort. In October 1915 he wrote his son Stefano, at that time a prisoner of war in an Austrian camp: "I feel that my whole life has been devoid of meaning; I no longer see any point in the things I do or the words I speak, and it astonishes me that there are others moving about outside this nightmare of mine and that they can act and speak. . . ."

Pirandello's personal doubts as to the nature of reality and the problem of identity—matters that were to occupy him all the rest of his life—were not at all the result of his early studies in German philosophy. His training was in philology. It was not until his late forties that he manifested any special interest in metaphysics or epistemology, and very likely at that time it was his personal problems that motivated his reading in those subjects. In 1915 he wrote Stefano that he was reading philosophy "and learning very little." His skeptical turn of mind manifested itself long before he came in contact with the writings of Kant or Hegel. *Pensaci, Giacomino!,* his first important play, was adapted from a *novella* he had published in 1910. It was not a work capable of carrying the philosophical superstructure of "transcendental farce," but it was a first-rate example of the Theatre of the Grotesque, and in it are contained in embryo most of the ideas that were to occupy him in his later drama. . . .

In Italy the world-wide interests in *Six Characters in Search of an Author* brought about a revaluation of Pirandello's work, and soon the groundwork was laid down for a serious study of his *oeuvre.* In his review of *Pensaci, Giacomino!* Adriano Tilgher had written, five years before the first production of *Six Characters:* "Pirandello's art is the art of leisure and amusement, without any profound content, without moral seriousness, without any vital interest in the mind and its problems. Fools may mistake for profundity the

ironic smile with which Pirandello presents his characters, but men of good
taste will not let themselves be deceived."

Pirandello's later plays caused Tilgher to alter his position. After the furor
attending the production of *Six Characters* he began to see in Pirandello's
works a clear reflection of his own ideas, and consequently a prime expression of the problems of the age. In the *Studi sul teatro contemporaneo,* which
he published in 1922, Tilgher devoted some sixty pages of text to an analysis
of Pirandello's ideas. In this essay he identified, under twenty-eight
sub-headings, all the themes which, in his opinion, Pirandello had so far
developed as a dramatic author. Among these were the questions of life and
form, appearance and reality, logic and the irrational, the inadequacy of
language, the question of identity, the question of truth, and the opposition
of the individual and society. The result of this detailed exegesis was to give
Pirandello a foremost place among those who were currently involved with
the intellectual life of Italy.

Adriano Tilgher was at this time at the height of his influence. He was
a Neapolitan of very decided views and of a distinctly militant disposition.
He was widely read, had come successively under the influence of
Schopenhauer, Dilthey, Bergson, and Georg Simmel, and was sharply opposed
to the historical school of criticism associated with Croce and Gentile. In
Tilgher's opinion Pirandello had a distinct affinity with Simmel, particularly
with respect to the duality of life and form. Tilgher wrote:

> All modern philosophy since Kant is founded on the deep intui-
> tion of the dualism that exists between Life, which is absolute
> spontaneity, creative activity, continual creation of the new and
> diverse, and the Forms, constructions, schemes, which tend to
> enclose it within itself, schemes which Life constantly destroys
> in order to go beyond them in its unwearied activity.

For Pirandello, in Tilgher's estimation, life was basically dramatic, and
the essence of this drama was the struggle between the primal nudity of life
and the clothes and masks with which "men pretend, and necessarily pretend, to clothe it." He continued:

> The philosophy implicit in Pirandello's art all centers on the funda-
> mental duality of Life and Form: Life perpetually mobile and fluid,
> which sinks and cannot help sinking into a form; yet profoundly
> opposes any form; and Form which, determining Life, while giv-
> ing rigid and precise limits to Life, freezes and kills its restless heat.

Pirandello's titles—"Naked Life," "Naked Masks"—according to Tilgher, make the underlying thought apparent. The nucleus of this thought is the intuition that every form is a definition and a limitation, and therefore a negation, of life. To think is to construct, to give form; consequently, as Bergson had indicated, to think is to limit and to suffocate life.

In this manner Tilgher propelled Pirandello directly into the forefront of the avant garde, and identified him with those Bergsonians who, considering logic to be an aberration of the mental faculties, looked to the intuition as the only access to truth. It was by no means Pirandello's idea. Pirandello was perhaps not too clear as to the validity of intuition, but he considered himself a logician. In *Il giuoco delle parti* he had Leone Gala beating an egg while he took Bergson severely to task for his assault on the power of reason:

> LEONE: I'm beating, I'm beating. . . . but just listen to me a moment! All that in our reality is fluid, living, mobile, dark, yes, I admit it, it escapes reason. . . . How it escapes reason, however, I cannot quite see, from the very fact that Signor Bergson can say it! How does he manage to say it? What makes him say it, if not reason? And so, it seems to me, it does not escape reason. Am I right? . . . Listen to me, Venanzi: it is a lovely jest, this that reason plays on Signor Bergson, making him believe that it is dethroned and humiliated by him, to the infinite delight of all the irrational ladies of Paris! Listen to me. According to him, reason.

And Leone launches into a discourse in dispraise of Bergson that is mercifully curtailed by his culinary activities.

But while he did not go along with Tilgher in the matter of the logical faculty, Pirandello found the theme of the duality of life and form entirely congenial. The idea that the individual has two contrary drives, the one dynamic and therefore resistant to fixation, the other static and opposed to change, was inherent in Pirandello's idea of drama from the beginning of his career. The vital flux and the forms it assumes were, in his view, in perpetual conflict, and in the individual psyche this conflict was a prime source of dramatic tension. This idea was developed in detail in a number of *novelle* long before the date of *Enrico IV,* and very fully in "La trappola" in 1912. In July 1922, soon after Tilgher's book came out, Pirandello told an interviewer for *L'Epoca*: "These ideas were mine alone; they had come spontaneously out of my spirit, they imposed themselves naturally on my thoughts. It was only afterwards, when my first dramatic works appeared, that I was told that these were the problems of the age, that others in this same period were troubled by them as I was."

Pirandello gratefully accepted Tilgher's formulation of his principles, but he was by no means ready to agree that he wrote from a formula. He wrote, he insisted, as an artist:

> My works are born of living images, the perennial source of art, but these images pass through the screen of concepts which have taken form in my mind. My works of art are never concepts trying to express themselves through images. Quite the contrary, they are images, often very vivid images of life, which through the operation of my mind assume universal significance by themselves, through the formal unity of art.

In his evaluation of Pirandello, Tilgher however defined him in accordance with more precise preconceptions. He saw him neither as a realist nor as an idealist in the Platonic sense. "Pirandello," he wrote,

> contemporary with the great spiritual and idealistic revolution in Italy and Europe at the beginning of the century, transports into art that anti-intellectualism and anti-rationalism which pervades all contemporary philosophy and which culminates in Relativism. Pirandello's art is anti-intellectual because it denies that any order of truth pre-exists, or that there are facts already determined of which thought has only to take account. It is, however, an art that affirms intellect insofar as it is full of the drama of the thinking thought which breasts the waves of the ocean of life and struggles to dominate it. Thought enters the paste of life and puts it in ferment. Therefore reality, which for other writers is monolithic, is for Pirandello broken and folded into planes which generate one another.

This was the rhetoric of Symbolism; and very likely these ideas pushed Pirandello somewhat further into the current of contemporary thought than he wished to go. The phrase *il pensiero pensante*—the thinking thought— was directly borrowed from Mallarmé's *ma pensée se pense*. The self-generating planes of reality recalled Jarry's "iridescent mental kaleidoscope." Pirandello did not normally use such language. His attitudes were certainly radical for the time, but his radicalism was closer to the Parnasse than to the Symbolists. As a philosophically minded writer he was very willing to negate reality, but as an artist he was rather inclined to observe nature than to destroy it. He had somehow blundered into Symbolism. Yet, like the painter

Nane Papa in the *novella* "Candelora," he was at bottom a Realist. Of Nane Papa he had written:

> All his life everything that was alive in him he had put, he had given, he had spent, for the pleasure of making a leaf seem fleshy, making himself into the fleshy paste, the fibre and vein of the leaf; or a stone, rigid and naked, so that it should feel and live as a stone on the canvas, and only this mattered to him.

There is no doubt that as an artist Pirandello was very much of Nane Papa's persuasion. It was indeed as a Realist that he had come to doubt reality, and in this respect he made common cause with the later Impressionists, the post-Impressionists. For him, as for them, the appearance of things was the ever-changing mask with which life was veiled; but life itself was unknown and indefinable, and Pirandello was more concerned with the mask than with what lay behind it. He himself had assumed the mask of a philosopher. It suited him badly. He was an artist and, at bottom, a Verist still. He was entirely willing to accept Pirandellism, now that it was coming into fashion. But he was never really a Pirandellian.

Nevertheless in accepting the system that Tilgher fathered on him, Pirandello found himself associated, willy-nilly, with all the various disruptive movements that were currently gnawing away at the bases of Western culture. He was no doubt in some degree a part of these himself. From the time of *Cosí è (se vi pare)* he might be considered a minister of disruption; but he was a minister without portfolio. He was so far not aligned with any movement. In an early essay entitled "Arte e coscienza d'oggi," published in 1893 when he was twenty-six, Pirandello had written:

> As the ancient norms have crumbled and the new are not yet sorted out or established, it is natural that the concept of the relativity of all things has so far extended itself in use as to make us lose our judgment of practically everything. . . . Never before, I think, has our life been ethically and aesthetically more broken up. Disconnected, without any principle of doctrine or faith, our thoughts whirl within the active drives that hang like clouds around a ruin. From this, it seems to me, derives the major part of our intellectual uneasiness.

Enrico IV, however, displayed something more than intellectual uneasiness. It was aggressively iconoclastic. But Pirandello's aggressiveness was not politically dangerous. What aroused his indignation was not the world order, but the absence of order in the world; not faith, but the impossibility

of faith. It is easy to understand the appeal of Mussolini's fascism to a man
of Pirandello's temper. He deplored its excesses, but fascism served to bind
together a world that was visibly falling to pieces and, much as he disliked
its methods, he preferred it to the political and moral chaos which preceded
it. His attacks upon the conventional acceptances of his time, its specious
truths and evanescent realities, were not those of a genuine nihilist, but those
of an outraged moralist. His nihilism, such as it was, was born of the contrast between the ideals he had inherited and the reality into which he was
thrust. It was the hypocrisy of those who tried to pass off the one for the
other that angered him. His fury was the fury of the 1860s, the high fury
of Garibaldi, not the cold madness of the 1920s.

Tilgher wrote of him, in a later article:

> Pirandello is a relativist. He denies the existence of objective reality
> and truth, and maintains that for each of us Being and Appearance
> are identical, that there is no such thing as knowledge, but only
> opinion (*Così è (se vi pare)*), and that one opinion is as good as
> another (*Ciascuno a suo modo*), precisely because for him all
> theories, affirmations, laws and norms are nothing but ephemeral
> forms within which life is momentarily trapped, in themselves
> ultimately devoid of truth and consistency.

This might well serve as a definition of *pirandellismo,* and from a superficial
reading of Pirandello such an inference might perhaps be drawn. But essentially his work does not support such a view. On the contrary, what is evident in his *novelle* and in his drama, from *Pensaci, Giacomino!* to *Enrico
IV,* is a clear affirmation of his faith in traditional principles—in justice, truth,
honesty, honor, and love—the solid virtues of middle-class culture, without
any trace of cynicism or doubt. It is, obviously, difficult to square these beliefs
with the skeptical and relativistic attitude he so often assumed; but Pirandello
made no special claim to consistency. In 1929 he wrote that though life and
form were fundamentally opposed, certain forms were indispensable to life:

> So long as forms remain alive, that is, so long as the vital force
> remains in them, they constitute a victory of the spirit. To destroy
> them simply in order to replace them with others is criminal. . . .
> Some forms are a natural expression of life itself. It is therefore
> impossible for them to become obsolete or to be replaced by
> others without destroying life in one of its true and natural
> manifestations.

Ultimately the position at which Pirandello arrived was not far removed from the position of Ibsen. The Pirandellians were bent on destroying the world, but Pirandello had no idea of abetting their efforts. He wished, on the contrary, to substitute the order of nature for the disorder of man's world. Reality, in his view, was the product of the human mind, not a system arbitrarily imposed on chaos by an omnipotent deity. It was therefore incumbent on mankind to devise a reality that would be appropriate to the human condition, and this reality would be subject to change as humanity improved its circumstances, morally and intellectually. His assault upon the cosmic order was, accordingly, intended to free humanity from the tyranny of the unreal. His doctrine was, so he believed, in the truest sense liberal and constructive. He was aware that it was generally misunderstood. In the interview published in *L'Epoca* in July 1922, in which he discussed Tilgher's analysis of his philosophy, Pirandello told the journalist: "What most people see in me is only the negative side of my thought. I seem to be a destructive devil who cuts the ground from under their feet. But surely the fact is the other way round. Before I pull the ground away, do I not show them where to put their feet?"

The truth is that all Pirandello's plays have a moral intention. But in the 1920s there was not much profit in being a moralist in the theatre. The pose of the destructive devil, the Satanist, the skeptic, had far greater glamor. Until he wrote *Six Characters in Search of an Author* Pirandello was pretty much in the mainstream of European drama. He had not advanced much beyond Ibsen's Dr. Stockman, and hardly as far as Shaw's Dick Dudgeon or Don Juan. In 1922 he was a radical writer in need of an intellectual affiliation, and when Tilgher offered him a post in the radical avant-garde, he hastened to accept it. The result was that he was drawn into relativism without really being a relativist, just as, some years later, he was drawn into fascism without being a fascist. At any rate, it is clear that, whether he agreed with it completely or not, he accepted Tilgher's formulation of his principles with gratitude, and in his future work went to some trouble to demonstrate its validity. After 1922 his articles and his lectures are resonant with phrases taken verbatim from Tilgher's book, and such plays as *Diana e la Tuda* are obviously composed in strict accord with Tilgher's recipe.

But Tilgher was not entirely laudatory in his evaluation of Pirandello. After elevating his plays to an intellectual level commensurate with his own, Tilgher went on to deplore Pirandello's excessive cerebrality. The dangers of drama conceived in the manner of Pirandello, he wrote, was its tendency toward an arid and intellectual excogitation. In his opinion, Pirandello's characters, and his situations, lacked variety: "It is undeniable that the Pirandellian characters resemble one another like drops of water: rather than different characters they seem to be one and the same character in situations that are always different and always the same." Moreover, he deplored the lack of balance between the grandiose metaphysical conception that the characters embodied and the meanness of their station. But, he added, Pirandello had not yet said his last word. In *Six Characters* and *Enrico IV* the metaphysical idea had more ample scope, and the familiar themes developed in a higher and rarer atmosphere. This was all preliminary work. There was, he concluded, bound to be a future masterpiece.

Immediately after the publication of Tilgher's book, Pirandello wrote him, expressing his gratitude for the service he had done him in clarifying his views. For a time he acted the part of the faithful disciple. But before long the affiliation became annoying, the more so as Tilgher insisted on posing publicly as his muse and mentor. Nevertheless their personal relations remained cordial until political considerations drove them apart. After Pirandello's association with the Fascist party, Tilgher, who was affiliated with an opposition paper, launched an attack against him, and their relations ended in bitter hostility.

It has been said that in furnishing Pirandello with a blueprint for his future work Tilgher did him a distinct disservice. In some measure this is true. But Tilgher came into his life at a time when Pirandello was in urgent need of a blueprint. In 1922 he was fifty-five, and he had worked at top speed for some thirty years without having time to take stock of his ideas. Tilgher furnished him with a precise inventory and assigned him a place in current thought. The idea that in accepting this form Pirandello lost his vitality has both glamor for the scholar and irony, but the facts do not bear it out. Tilgher provided a mirror in which Pirandello could see himself, and Pirandello was keenly aware that to see oneself is dangerous; for at this point, as he often wrote, life stops and thought begins. But Pirandello did not by any means stop living in his fifties, either as a man or as an artist. On the contrary, in these years his activity was immeasurably enhanced. It was as if he had gained a second hold on youth, and he developed impressively in every direction. He became a power in the theatre, a manager, a stage director; and nationally a man of consequence, a senator and a Nobel laureate. But he wrote nothing finer than the two great works of the 1920s. His future masterpiece was in the past. It needed only to be revalued. This happened.

The aging poet in *Quando si è qualcuno* resigns himself to the tragedy of success, stifling, for the benefit of his family and his friends, the vital impulse that stirs once again in his veins. But while it is tempting to identify this monumental figure with Pirandello, there is no close relation between them. With time—it has often been noted—human genius tends to crystallize in intelligible forms. After 1922 Pirandello became "*qualcuno*"—a Somebody. It was perhaps not an altogether enviable fate; but Pirandello could hardly complain. It was the goal to which he had aspired all his life. He had attained it, and it was sad for him; but not as sad, perhaps, as if he had not attained it.

Until quite recently almost everything that has been said of Pirandello by way of interpretation has echoed Tilgher's analysis, so that Pirandello's work has been thought of principally in terms of the duality of life and form, and his style has been decried for its cerebral quality. In truth, most of Pirandello's plays hardly involve the contrast of life and form, and his style is rather melodramatic and passionate than cerebral. Many of his plays require, it is true, the services of a *raisonneur,* sometimes an intrusive character such as Laudisi in *Cosí è (se vi pare),* sometimes one who is an active protagonist such as Baldovino in *Il piacere dell'onestà,* Ciampa in *Il berretto a sonagli,* the Father in *Sei personaggi in cerca d'autore,* or the madman in *Enrico IV.* These characters talk a great deal, and unquestionably they served the author as useful intellectual vehicles. But only in an age when the drama was expected to provide grandiose displays of passion could Pirandello's plays be called "arid intellectual excogitations." By 1922 Shaw had amply demonstrated the dramatic possibilities of intellectual discussion, and in England his plays were respected as entertaining doctrinal demonstrations. But in Italy in this period the theatre was not expected to serve such purposes. It would be thirty years before an audience would be carried away so far as to consider dialectic a form of poetry.

There is, as a matter of fact, not much that can be called poetry in Pirandello's dialectic. What is poetic in his plays is not their logic, but the absence of logic. In Pirandello's plays reason is a purely defensive device. It is the armored shell which shelters the naked creature that lives in it, the refuge the character constructs to protect itself from the world outside. The dialectic is, moreover, seldom convincing. But it is invariably touching. Compared with Shaw's magisterial debaters, Pirandello's logicians are poor things, by turns comic and pathetic, and the philosophical mask that they affect, even in its most rigid forms, never quite serves to conceal the contoured face behind it. Leone Gala is a stoic with a good stomach, but for all the ingenuity of his rationalization, he cannot manage to digest his bitterness.

Pirandello's crowning masterpiece, which Tilgher so confidently predicted, did not in fact materialize. But, taken together, the twenty-one plays that followed *Enrico IV* almost compensated for its absence. Some were of prime importance; none was altogether negligible; all in all, it was a masterly achievement. In these later plays the dominant theme, expressed in a wide variety of situations, is the illusory nature of what passes for reality, so that, by the time he had done with it, Pirandello's world was in shreds. When he began work on his last play, *I giganti della montagna* (1936), the chief wonder of the modern world was that it was still intact.

Soon after finishing *Enrico IV* Pirandello wrote one of his most successful plays, *Vestire gli ignudi* (*To Clothe the Naked* [1923]). It is of classic design, and unfolds retrospectively an action that extends back some months before the play begins and resolves it in the space of a day. In the construction of this play there is some hint of *Six Characters;* but in this case it is an author who goes in search of a character, and the action concerns the efforts of the protagonist to give the world, through the author, a becoming account of her life.

At the beginning of the play Ersilia Drei has drawn attention to herself in Rome by attempting suicide in a public park. She lands in a hospital, and a journalist who comes to interview her publishes the story of her life in his paper. The novelist Lodovico Nota is so deeply impressed with this story that he takes Ersilia to his home, intending to work her life story into a novel. Her story, in fact, reads like the libretto of a sentimental opera. She was employed as governess in the house of the Italian consul in Smyrna. A naval lieutenant won her heart and, after he promised to marry her, she gave herself to him. But Lieutenant Franco, in the way of naval officers, never came back. The girl was disgraced. Then the consul's child had an accident and was killed. The blame fell on Ersilia. She was dismissed. In despair, she came to Rome in search of her lover, only to find that he was about to marry another. Now quite hopeless, she gave herself to the first man she met and, in her revulsion, took poison.

This story, when it is published, makes a deep impression in Rome. The naval officer, now a civilian, renounces his engagement and hastens to make good his promise to Ersilia. She rejects him. Then the consul appears. He is furious. Bit by bit the facts of the case come out. The consul is actually a kindly man married to a sickly wife who has had much reason for jealousy. Ersilia, after having been seduced by Franco, became the consul's mistress. At the time of the child's fatal accident, the two lovers were surprised together by the jealous wife. There was a scene, and Ersilia was dismissed at the wife's insistence. Later, in Rome, alone and with no means of support, she tried to earn a living on the streets. Failing that, she took poison. Afterwards, in the hospital, sure that she was on her deathbed, she told the reporter the romantic tale that was published in the press.

In her present circumstances Ersilia refuses to have anything further to do with any of the men around her—neither with the novelist who desires to romanticize her tale, nor with the naval gentleman who offers to marry her, nor with the consul who now wishes to have her back with him. She wishes only to finish dying. In the end she manages that by taking another dose of poison. This time it is effective.

A play couched in these terms might easily lapse into sentimentality, but Pirandello saved it from mawkishness by giving Ersilia Drei a singularly strong and resolute character. She is nothing, she tells them, a lump of clay modeled by chance, without any personality of her own. In fact, she displays such nobility of character that she dwarfs the men who, more or less unwittingly, have collaborated to destroy her. The men are, indeed, pitiful creatures, and the scene in which they wrangle among themselves over the dying girl is sufficiently comic to give a grotesque tinge to what is essentially a tragic situation. Franco, jealous of his honor, offers to fight the consul because he suspects him of having seduced Ersilia before he did. The consul is worried about his reputation and denies having had any relations whatever with the girl. The father of Franco's bride insists that his daughter's marriage must take place at any cost. The novelist and the journalist try desperately to extricate themselves from a situation which promises to be professionally embarrassing. In the midst of these noises Ersilia appears, pale, dying, and completely dignified. Her curtain speech is in the nature of an aria. In all her life, she tells them, she had never been able to put on a decent dress without some dog tearing it away from her. Now the dogs are at her again. Her pathetic attempt to find a dress to cover her nakedness even now has been denied:

> I wished to make myself a nice one to die in—the nicest—the one I had always dreamed of—and which was also torn away—a bride's dress—but only to die in, to die in, to die in, and no more—So—with a few tears of sympathy—and no more. Well, no! No! No! I wasn't allowed even this. Torn off my back, stripped off, even this! No! To die naked! Uncovered, humiliated, despised! Well, there we are—are you satisfied? And now go away, go! Let me die quietly, naked—.

The portrait of the aging writer Lodovico Nota is interesting. He is by no means a sympathetic character. Like the naval officer Franco, the consul, and the journalist, he is a self-centered man who sees in Ersilia mainly a subject for exploitation. He is made to say that Pirandello's work fills him with loathing. It is amusing, therefore, that the manner in which he is described suggests that he is a caricature of the author himself,

> a handsome man of commanding appearance, although he has

passed his fiftieth year. Piercing eyes, sparkling, and on his still fresh lips an almost youthful smile. Cold, reflective, entirely deprived of those natural gifts which win sympathy and confidence, unsuccessful in stimulating any warmth of emotion, he tries to appear at least affable, but this affability which is intended to seem spontaneous and is not, instead of reassuring, disturbs, and is sometimes disconcerting.

Lodovico Nota is an honest craftsman, a realist and an ironist. Ersilia's true story is, in his opinion, incomparably more beautiful than the romantic tale he had at first intended to compose, and it is more deeply comic. It is inevitable also that in these circumstances Lodovico should play the Pirandellian *raissoneur:*

> The facts! The facts! My dear sir, the facts are what you assume
> them to be and, therefore, in the mind there are no facts, there
> is only life that appears sometimes this way and sometimes that.
> The facts are the past. When the soul recedes—you said it your-
> self—and life abandons it. I have no faith in facts.

Lodovico Nota goes a step further than Lamberto Laudisi in his scepticism, but the situation in *Vestire gli ignudi* does not center on the question of truth. The question here is one of psychology. In Ersilia's case the facts are not long in doubt. She has been telling lies, evidently, and she admits it readily—lies not for profit, but for cosmetic reasons. She has adorned herself with pretty lies in order to die decently. When her pathetic subterfuge is discovered, the issue, insofar as the facts are concerned, is settled. From a philosophic viewpoint the problem on which the play concentrates is the relation of life and form, the problem of the Theatre of the Grotesque. The assumption is that, in general, life inclines to beauty and strives to create harmonious forms. The form to which Ersilia aspires, her ideal, is that of a *fidanzata,* a bride-to-be. It is supremely ironical that for a woman in her position life can offer nothing more beautiful than the prospect of marriage. But the fact is that the wedding day is, for her, the summit of earthly happiness, the culmination of her dreams, the one enviable moment of existence, and in the moment of death she longs to clothe herself in this beauty.

Ersilia is denied this happiness. It is pathetic that in the end she is not permitted to embellish herself suitably. It is even more pathetic that she should wish to do so. In death, as in life, what is important is not the reality, but the appearance of things; and one can sympathize readily with the girl's wish to look nice even for a moment before her life is forever extinguished, at the same time that the irony of the situation puts her death in a grimly comic light. In Pirandello's canon there is no better example of the Grotesque.

For the rest, Ersilia is the victim of her environment. She has been exploited not by villains, but by ordinary, well-meaning people in the ordinary course of business. There is no one to blame for her misfortunes, least of all herself, and there is nothing said in this play of a social system which sees women chiefly as a means of reproducing the race. This play doubtless involves some measure of social criticism, but Pirandello was not energetic as a social reformer: the play speaks for itself. Ersilia Drei makes one ashamed of humanity; but her play offers no remedies. It is, at best, a gesture of despair.

Vestire gli ignudi is certainly one of Pirandello's finest plays. It made a profound impression. In Rome the part of Ersilia Drei was played by Maria Melato, and by Emma Grammatica in Milan. Ruggero Ruggeri produced the play in Torino. The following year Pirandello produced *La vita che ti diedi* (*The Life I Gave You* [1924]). He had written it with Eleanora Duse in mind for the role of the devoted mother who keeps her dead son alive in fantasy, and Duse in fact agreed to do it. But Duse was closely identified with D'Annunzio. She postponed the rehearsals on various pretexts and at last withdrew from the venture. She was wise.

The theme of *La vita che ti diedi* was one of Pirandello's favorites. He had used it in several *novelle,* in "La camera in attesa," in "I pensionati della memoria," and quite recently in "Notizia del mondo," which was published in 1922. The play is said to have been Pirandello's favorite play. It has to do, at least in theory, with the power of the imagination to create a reality. It is in fact a celebration of mother love, very touching, but somewhat too sentimental to be revived, and it was no great success even in its original production. It was followed, the following year, in May 1924, by *Ciascuno a suo modo,* a most ambitious experiment.

By this time Pirandello was in every sense a professional showman. He had never been averse to publicity. Now he threw himself into the role of the intellectual mountebank with all the fervor of one who had been forced to bottle up his natural exhibitionism the better part of his life. *Ciascuno a suo modo* (*Each in His Way*) made a new departure in the theatre, and Pirandello was resolved to make the most of it. The text, published by Bemporad, was made available some days before the opening. It served the influential critic of *La Gazzetta del Popolo* of Turin, Domenico Lanza, as the basis of a spirited attack on Pirandello and everything that Pirandello stood for in the theatre. Pirandello countered with an equally vigorous article in the Milanese *Corriere della Sera.* There were other explosions in the Italian press and, amid all the hubbub, the play opened in Milan before a capacity audience at an advanced scale of prices. Pirandello had gone so far as to plant actors in the house with instructions to create a commotion in classic style. But the thing had been overdone. To the author's extreme disappointment the play was received with respect. There was applause at the end, but neither catcalls nor brawls. When the play was over the audience left the theatre, evidently chastened, but not excited.

Pirandello subtitled this play *Commedia a chiave* (*A Play with a Key*). The key is supplied by the play itself. The action involves an imaginary situation which is based, supposedly, on an exactly analogous situation which is supposed to be real, and is documented by news reports distributed to the audience as it enters the theatre. Pirandello's play thus represents on the stage with fictitious names the consequences of a sensational affair which—we are urged to imagine—actually took place and was widely reported in the press. The people who were "actually" involved in the suicide of the young sculptor Giacomo la Vela—the actress Amelia Moreno and Baron Nuti—have come to see the play that has been written about them, and are seated in the audience with their friends. The action thus takes place on two planes of being which mirror one another. In fact, of course, neither is real; so that the audience is required to distinguish reality on three levels—its own, the presumed reality of Moreno and Nuti, and the drama of their counterparts on the stage. Difficult as this seems, it presents no difficulty at all in the theatre.

The plot of *Ciascuno a suo modo* is extremely complex. The curtain rises on an upper-class salon. It transpires that Doro Palegari and his friend Francesco have had a violent disagreement regarding an actress called Delia Morello, whom neither has met. Delia is notorious for her many lovers. On the eve of her marriage to the gifted young sculptor Giorgio Salvi, she was found by her fiancé in the arms of his friend Michele Rocca, who was engaged to his sister. As a result Giorgio shot himself. The scandal has since stirred discussion throughout Italy.

In arguing the pros and cons of this affair Doro and Francesco have almost come to blows. But Doro, who had originally defended the lady, now sees the matter in a different light. The same thing has happened to Francesco. Since each has reversed his opinion, the two are once again at loggerheads, and this time Doro insults his friend so thoroughly that he provokes him to a challenge. At this point the actress Delia Morello appears. She has come to thank Doro for defending her so warmly and, since he has taken her part so confidently, while she herself is confused, she asks him to help her clarify her motives in acting as she did.

Evidently Doro understands her better than she understands herself. In the ensuing scene, by means of a series of curiously linked speeches, Doro and Delia evolve a theory that thoroughly satisfies them. Delia, they decide, is a female Don Juan, a *femme fatale* engaged in a vendetta against all men. Men have so far considered only her body. She has found this humiliating and has reacted by systematically arousing them and then frustrating their desires. The sculptor Salvi, however, was not attracted to her physically. He was concerned only with her form, from which he was modeling a figure. But Delia found his objectivity irritating: "An angel is always more irritating to a woman than a beast." She did her best, therefore, to excite his passions. When she succeeded in this, as was her custom, she denied herself to him. The result was a proposal of marriage. She had no intention of marrying him; but she asserted her power by forcing him to present her—a notorious woman—to his mother and his sister. The sister's fiancé, Michele Rocca, was violently opposed to Salvi's marriage. It was, however, only to rid herself of Salvi that she contrived to have him surprise her in his studio with Rocca.

Doro understands that Delia has no malice. She merely manifests the vital spirit, flowing from one form into another, playing as many parts in life as she does in the theatre, in the vain hope always of finding out one day what she is in reality. Francesco has a quite different idea. In his opinion Delia is a vulgar adventuress, using her charms in order to advance herself in society. Thus when she discovered in Rocca the chief obstacle to her marriage to Salvi, she proceeded to seduce him in order to expose his hypocrisy and so to discredit him. To Doro's extreme surprise Delia concedes that this interpretation may also be true. He is now completely confused. He has provoked a duel with his best friend: "For what? For something that nobody understands—what it is, how it is—neither I, nor he, and not even she herself!" The curtain falls on this effect.

It rises at once on "The First Choral Interlude." The scene now represents the corridor at the rear of the auditorium. People are leaving their seats for the entr'acte. The stage direction goes so far as to indicate the behavior of the audience:

> It is nowadays known to all that at each act curtain in the irritating plays of Pirandello there will necessarily be discussions and disagreements. Let those who defend him assume before their intractable adversaries that smiling humility which always has the marvellous effect of irritating them beyond endurance.

Following this suggestion, the interlude consists of a heated critical discussion carried on by actors costumed as spectators, so that the audience is invited to view itself on the stage in the act of arguing heatedly over the situation it has just witnessed.

In the second act, while a fencing master is preparing Francesco for his forthcoming encounter with Doro, Diego Cinci takes the opportunity to deliver a lecture on the difficulty of knowing oneself. For social purposes, he says, we construct some sort of personality, a form that will represent us to the world, and this fiction regulates our behavior. But in a critical moment we may see the whole façade we have erected crumble before the vital current that flows through us without our being aware of it:

> Put aside the little puppet you construct, with the feigned inter-
> pretation of your acts and feelings, and you will soon see that
> it has nothing to do with what you really are, or can be, with
> what is in you of which you are not aware. You will see that this
> is a terrible god, and woe to you if you oppose him; but this god
> becomes a compassionate being ready to forgive your every fault
> if you simply abandon yourself to him, and stop trying to justify
> yourself.

His homily is interrupted by the entrance of Michele Rocca. He comes with still another explanation of Delia's behavior, and also with another challenge. The reason he betrayed his beloved friend, he says, was to discredit the shameless woman his friend intended to marry. Therefore he must fight the man who dares to justify Delia, and who thus impugns his honor. It turns out that this man is now Francesco. In these circumstances Francesco refuses to fight Doro, and offers to fight Rocca instead. The seconds are outraged, and begin to quarrel. Then Delia comes in and rushes into Rocca's arms. As the two go off lovingly together, the truth at last becomes manifest to all. Delia and Rocca were in love from the beginning. They falsified their true motives for themselves and for the world in order to give some rational basis to their passion. The play makes its point: we mask the natural impulse—which is insuperable—by inventing fictions in conformity with the social forms to which we are subject.

The point is doubtless valid; but as drama the play leaves much to be desired. The recognition scene, with its peripeteia, is needlessly exaggerated. In order that we may see Life, in all its madness, bursting through the cultural veil that normally conceals it, Rocca and Delia are made to act like wild beasts mating in the jungle. The scene is embarrassing; but for all its clumsiness, it makes its point. As these lovers embrace and run off, presumably to copulate, Francesco makes an appropriate comment:

FRANCESCO: But they are two lunatics.
DIEGO: Take a look at yourself.

This speech brings down the curtain. It goes up immediately on the "Second Choral Interlude," which is intended to represent the effect of the second act on the audience. The effect is, in theory, electric. The real-life protagonist, Amelia Moreno, breaks away from her friends and rushes up to the stage, which is now depicted in reverse. Applause, boos, and sounds of tumult come from the auditorium backstage. La Moreno appears to have slapped someone in her fury—who it was, exactly, is not clear. Then, amid wild excitement, she and Baron Nuti—Rocca's real-life prototype—repeat the scene they have just witnessed, this time in "reality," and run out of the theatre together. There was to have been a third act. But the actors are by now thoroughly disturbed. They refuse to go on. The curtain is lowered. The *capocomico* appears before it and announces to the audience—this time the real audience—that the play cannot continue.

For all its seeming novelty the situation in *Ciascuno a suo modo* is a variation of the *dubbio* of *Così è (se vi pare)*. The technique is an extension of the technique of *Sei personaggi in cerca d'autore*. In *Così è (se vi pare)* Laudisi drives home the idea that truth is a matter of opinion, a conclusion which has much in its favor, but is not the point of the play. In *Ciascuno a suo modo the raisonneur* is Diego Cinci, a character who demonstrates logically that it is impossible to discover the true motives of people's actions. His argument, also, has not much to do with the play, for in the end the true motive for the behavior of the characters is made clear. The play is thus mainly a drama of mask and face, and only incidentally a demonstration of the relativity of truth.

The dramatic framework that encloses the action of *Ciascuno a suo modo* is in many respects similar to that of *Sei personaggi in cerca d'autore*. The difference is that in the present case the characters are presumed to be real people seated in the audience, while the actors who depict them move about on the stage. Moreover the action on the stage does not falsify the "real" action. On the contrary, it is by seeing themselves objectified on the stage in the roles they played in real life that Amelia Moreno and Baron Nuti come to realize why they behaved as they did, and it is this realization that brings about their reconciliation in real life. Thus *Ciascuno a suo modo* is in effect an exercise in psychotherapy, a revelation of repressed wishes through dramatic projection.

The technical innovation, however, through which Pirandello undertook to motivate and control the behavior of the audience as well as the business

of the actors, was largely ineffective. The device was perhaps suggested by
the technique of *Fanny's First Play* (1911), in which Shaw caricatured his
critics by putting them in the audience of the play-within-play, where he made
himself the subject of discussion. Pirandello, in similar fashion, put his
principal adversary, the critic Lanza, on the stage. But Pirandello's touch was
heavy, and the effort at self-advertisement is painfully evident. His attempts
to stir up the audience, also, were misdirected. Evidently the audience did
not enjoy seeing itself caricatured on the stage. At the first performance of
Six Characters in Rome, the scandal was, by all accounts, spontaneous; and,
in spite of its effect on his nerves, it did much to establish Pirandello's
reputation as a provocative author. It was probably naive to engineer a
repetition three years later, and, predictably, it did not work. There was
obviously no need for the paying guests to stir themselves up about a play
when there were actors present who were paid to do it for them. As it turned
out, the actors were excited. The audience was calm.

The principle, nevertheless, was interesting, and was destined to have
interesting consequences. There was, of course, nothing new in putting a
fictitious audience on the stage. It was a device familiar to Shakespeare. Actors
had been put in the audience from the time of Beaumont and Fletcher's *The
Knight of the Burning Pestle* (1613); but no one could have predicted the
effect of *Ciascuno a suo modo* on the development of the drama in the
following years. As it happened, the moment was critical and, in putting this
play on the stage at this time, Pirandello indicated the direction of a whole
new movement in the theatre.

The Milanese production of *Ciascuno a suo modo* was accounted a
success, but the play was not produced again in Italy in Pirandello's lifetime.
When Pitoëff produced it in Paris two years later, the more conservative critics
considered it a piece of effrontery in questionable taste, but it soon became
evident that, whatever its merits as drama, this play implied a wholly new
conception of theatre. Among other things, it rejected the idea of the stage
as a reality apart from the reality of everyday life, together with the realistic
tradition that the Théâtre-libre had so carefully nurtured. In this play the fourth
wall, seemingly impenetrable, which had so long divided the play from the
audience, was suddenly whisked away, and the reality of the stage was merged
with the reality of the people who sat before it. Henceforth the auditorium
no longer offered a safe refuge from the author's fantasy. It was enclosed
in it. The play could therefore take on the seriousness of a real experience,
and the audience sat in the playhouse at its peril.

It was difficult, obviously, to go much further in this direction without
endangering the very idea of theatre, which accords the events depicted on

the stage an enhanced reality in virtue of their fictional character. There were those, nevertheless—among them Artaud and Brecht—who were eager to take the risk. Thus the techniques of *Ciascuno a suo modo* contributed a good deal to the theory of The Theatre of Cruelty—the First Manifesto was published in 1932—and to the Brechtian experiments with *Verfremdung* about 1936.

S U S A N   B A S S N E T T - M c G U I R E

The Myth Plays

In addition to the theatre-in-the-theatre trilogy, Pirandello grouped together three more plays, under the heading of *modern myths*. These three are *The New Colony*, the social myth, *Lazarus*, the religious myth and *The Mountain Giants*, the myth of art. To these three, Bragaglia adds two more: the one-act play, *La sagra del Signore della nave* (*The Festival of Our Lord of the Ship*), 1925, and *La favola del figlio cambiato* (*The Changeling*), 1938, myths of temporality and maternity.

By using the term "myth" Pirandello clearly set out to indicate that in these works he was trying to do something different. In an interview with Alberto Cecchi in 1928 Pirandello explained that he wanted to address all mortal creatures in his work. "Tragedy," Pirandello declared, "is always mythical. It has its beginning and end on the stage. The origins of myths are these: the elementary events of earthly cycles, dawns, sunsets, births, deaths." Pirandello was moving towards a notion of theatre that would provide the audience not only with something to see and discuss, but with something to experience directly. In his theatre of myth, the *coup de théâtre* is overtaken by the idea of the miracle, which actors and audiences share alike. What Pirandello was aiming for was a transcendent theatre, where the debate between life and art that had dominated much of his earlier writing would be subsumed into a new, global experience-theatre. In his short but important piece on Pirandello's theatre of myth, Sandro d'Amico refers to Julian Beck of the Living Theatre who had declared *The Mountain Giants* to be the climax of Pirandello's metatheatre. For in this last of his myths, Pirandello had attempted to tackle the vast problem of the impossibility of

From *Luigi Pirandello*. © 1983 by Susan Bassnett-McGuire. Grove Press, 1983.

communication *and* the impossibility of producing theatre; in this sense the myths should be seen as a culmination of Pirandello's play-writing career, rather than as a decline into para-religious senility. D'Amico also suggests that the myths

> probably arose out of a need to clarify his own work and to give it a unity with the themes already apparent in his preceding works, such as charity, motherhood, sacrifice and pain.

The parallels with Julian Beck, Luis Valdez and, more obviously, Grotowski, to name but three major post-war theatre innovators, may serve to further stress the importance of Pirandello's myths. For perhaps even more radically than in his theatre trilogy, Pirandello was endeavouring to produce a new type of theatre, to add a dimension to the whole process of theatre making. That the myths were never popular and have been largely ignored by directors and critics is another matter. They remain to be rediscovered, and their significance is well summed up by Giovanni Sinicropi, when he states that

> Pirandello's endeavour as man and artist closes thus with the recognition of the impossibility of bridging the gap between art and life. The last act of his creation had aimed at crossing that abyss; and even though he managed to reduce it to a small size, easily covered at one jump, it could never be filled up. The leap into the irrational area of myth does not have to derive from a sense of renunciation, but one of achievement, of a necessary completion of the artist's aspirations.

THE NEW COLONY

When this play was first staged, at the Teatro Argentina in Rome in 1928, with Marta Abba in the role of La Spera, both Abba's performance and Pirandello's direction were heavily criticized. However, the play itself was considered to be good, and the reviewer in the *Corriere della Sera* declared it to be the "least melancholy and most hopeful play" of Pirandello's entire output.

The New Colony is a very long play, having three acts and a Prologue, and has an extended cast list. Moreover, its staging requires both indoor and outdoor sets, and these factors have no doubt contributed to the scarcity of revivals. It is cumbersome to stage and expensive and would require careful handling to hold the huge cast together. It has only been revived twice in Italy since the original staging.

The Prologue serves to introduce the main characters and to present the world of corruption from which they try to escape. The scene is set in Nuccio's tavern, and we are introduced immediately to a clash of wills between Padron Nocio, the local landowner, and Tobba, an old fisherman. Padron Nocio emerges as a Brechtian villain, a symbol of the corruption of power and wealth, who accuses Tobba of putting crazy notions into his son Doro's head:

> PADRON NOCIO: You shouldn't go messing around with my son's ideas. . . .
> TOBBA: Who me?
> PADRON NOCIO: Yes, you, talking to him about your island. May God sink the blasted thing!
> TOBBA: (*as though he expected something different*) Oh, the island.
> (*Smiling*)
> The paradise of wicked men.

The idea of the island, of the place of refuge where the evils of the world can be avoided is thus introduced in the opening moments of the play. Later in the Prologue, when the dissatisfaction of the poor fishermen, who eke out their livelihood by smuggling and live in constant fear of the law, has reached its climax, the idea of the island is brought up again. This time it is introduced by La Spera, the local whore whose lover, Currao, is one of the smugglers. La Spera has not been brutalized by her existence as some of the men have been, and she still has enough spirit to want to escape. She suggests flight to Tobba's island, and when the others refer to the belief that the island will one day sink into the ocean, La Spera convinces them with her enthusiasm:

> CURRAO (*thinking*): Go back to the island?
> LA SPERA: It'll be our liberation.
> FILACCIONE: Right! when you sink under the sea with it.
> LA SPERA: And where are you here? haven't you sunk low enough already? You couldn't sink any lower than here. But at least it'll be God that pushes you under instead of men even wickeder than you are. They're wickeder because they won't even let you come up for air for a second just to breathe.

The island the smugglers go to is a former penal colony that has been abandoned because it was said to be gradually sinking into the sea. But to the wretched people of the mainland, led by La Spera and Currao, the image of the island becomes one of hope (the name *Spera* means hope), for here they plan to build a new society, freed from the shackles of the previous one.

As the Prologue ends, La Spera appears holding her child, the baby son without whom she will not leave, and tells the others that a miracle has occurred—she is suddenly able to breastfeed her own child. Tobba speaks the final words of the scene, warning the company that this is truly a sign from God, an indication that He will guide them and protect them, and in the final tableau all kneel in prayer.

Act 1 is set on the island, and it is immediately apparent that the promise of a new life has not been fulfilled. Because La Spera is the only woman on the island, the other men lust after her, and Currao, who has become their leader, uses his relationship with her to assert his power over the others. La Spera, the despised local whore in her previous life, is now the queen of the island, and her joy of motherhood causes her to be reborn in moral terms: she becomes a truly pure woman, the source of all positive values in the new society. The quarrels between the island's new colonists intensify, and when one of them dies of a heart attack at the end of act 1, the tableau is in marked contrast to the end of the Prologue. For as the man lies dead, a symbol of the failure of the attempt to create a new life, only some of them kneel. Belief in God has begun to fade.

In act 2, the forces of disintegration receive new help with the arrival of Padron Nocio from the mainland, bringing with him other women, including his daughter, Mita. Padron Nocio sets up a deal with Currao in an attempt to share the control of the new colony. La Spera's growing isolation is symbolized by the concluding moments of the act, when she sits alone with her child, refusing to accept solitude, telling the baby that they belong to each other.

The deal between Padron Nocio and Currao involves the marriage of Currao with Mita and the necessary abandoning of La Spera. Confused and lonely, La Spera resists attempts to make her give up her child to Currao, who is claiming the rights of fatherhood; in the final climax of the play she tries to prevent what she believes is an attack on the life of Doro, the young boy she has befriended. With the coming of Padron Nocio, La Spera's new status has been destroyed, and she is again treated as a whore. Clinging to her child, a symbolic figure of love and charity, she is insulted by the crowd who urge Currao on to pull the baby out of her arms. In despair, La Spera cries out that if he takes the child from her, "the earth will quake," and the force of her belief makes this happen. The play ends with the cataclysmic swallowing up of the island by the sea. Out of the total destruction that ensues, only La Spera is left, with her child. The play ends with the image of La Spera and the child alone above the flood waters.

The New Colony is a play about the corruption of society, a corruption that men carry with them wherever they go. But although the play ends with the great destructive flood, the figure of La Spera represents a belief in an ideal. For La Spera is an indication of the *possibility* of change and the mere existence of that possibility gives hope. In act 1, when Currao declares that he knows the child is his, La Spera voices her hopes that a new life really is possible:

> If it were really true that coming here and changing our lives means
> that we'll all become different people from what we used to be.

In contrast to her hope, the others refer constantly back to the life they once knew, either because they resent the loss of certain things or because they resent the changes that have come about. Their grievances focus on La Spera, the living proof that change can take place; only because of her newfound strength is she able to deal with the way in which her past immorality is thrown back at her. In an important scene with Currao in act 2, the contrast between the strength La Spera gains through change and Currao's fears of the past emerges most clearly. La Spera tells Currao that her strength comes from the innocent faith of her child, whose love makes the evils of her past life seem like a bad dream.

> CURRAO: But he'll find out. . . . Tomorrow he'll find out. . . .
> LA SPERA: I'll teach him what he needs to know.
> CURRAO: If only there weren't other people.

But of course those other people do exist, and in the end Currao proves himself to be as corruptible as any of them. What remains untainted is La Spera's love and faith, and it is because of that love that in the final holocaust she is saved.

Unlike so many of his plays, which have bourgeois protagonists, the characters of *The New Colony*, like the characters in *Liolà*, are poor, low-life figures. The language used is rich and colourful, and their coarse vitality is explicitly portrayed, but they are presented as bestial figures, in dark contrast to La Spera whose Madonna-like image grows through the play. Whereas in *Liolà*, the world of the Sicilian village was used to give a sense of exuberance, in *The New Colony* the world of poor fishermen is used to show the depths of human degradation.

The New Colony lends itself readily to comparison with Brecht's *The Caucasian Chalk Circle*, where mother-love also emerges triumphant in a world of corruption. But although there may be superficial similarities, the gap between the Fascist playwright and the Marxist playwright looms large. Brecht shows the crisis of society as deriving from class struggle and from unequal distribution of wealth and power, and his plays are not empirical but dialectic. In Brecht's play, as in Pirandello's, the audience is on the side of the female protagonist in her struggles against the forces that seek to crush her, but in Brecht's play the heroine wins through and keeps the child she has saved because she acts in accordance with her natural instincts of love, and the judge rules in her favour. Her solution is thus brought about *by* society and by its laws, whereas in *The New Colony* there is no such solution. La Spera is saved by an act of God, by a *deus ex machina* that sweeps away her tormentors. She is not saved by reason or by love, nor by any of the forces that should go to making a new society, but by a completely irrational act that supposedly has divine origins. In this final *coup de théâtre* the extent of Pirandello's lack of commitment becomes apparent: the final miracle is superhuman and only reinforces the image of man's helplessness. With such a world view, there can be no new society, for Pirandello's characters do not have the capacity to work out a solution for themselves. . . .

THE MOUNTAIN GIANTS

Pirandello began writing *The Mountain Giants* in 1929 but had still not finished the play by the time of his death in 1936. It was performed one year later in 1937 in the Boboli Gardens in Florence, but unquestionably the most famous production of this play was the version directed by Giorgio Strehler at the Teatro Lirico, Milan, in 1967. Pirandello's son, Stefano, has put together details of the unwritten final act and, as Strehler points out in his programme note, the unwritten end "offers the possibility of transforming a work," an extraordinary opportunity for any director.

The Mountain Giants is one of Pirandello's most important works and yet it is also one of the least known outside Italy. He described it in a letter to Marta Abba as his masterpiece, explaining also that

> The mountain giants are the triumph of fantasy, the triumph of poetry, but at the same time also the tragedy of poetry in this brutal, modern world.

The play may be seen as a statement of Pirandello's disillusionment with the role of art in contemporary society, a position towards which he had been moving steadily for many years. Pirandello had deeply involved himself in exploring the apparent dichotomy between art and life, between form and motion, and had come increasingly to investigate this duality in theatre terms, and yet at the same time he had sought the illusory ideal solution offered by the ideology of Fascism. The incompatibility between these two viewpoints accounts for the increasing sense of tension and uneasiness in Pirandello's writing in the late 1920s and early 1930s, and nowhere is that tension expressed more powerfully and explicitly than in *The Mountain Giants*.

In this play all notion of a naturalistic setting has disappeared. The action takes place in a surreal world, in the fantastic villa Scalogna inhabited by a grotesque group of mad people, led by Cotrone a wizard and illusionist. Into this group come a company of traveling actors who, driven by Ilse, the leading lady, are trying to popularize the posthumous work of a young poet who killed himself for love of her. The title of this work is *The Changeling*, and when the actors begin to perform it in section 3 (the missing section would have been section 4), we realize that it is indeed Pirandello's own play of the same name. Cotrone proposes to the company that they should present their play for the wedding festivities of the mountain giants and, in the missing final section, they agree to this. A makeshift stage is rigged up with a curtain round a tree, in an open space in front of the Giants' houses, and the actors prepare for their play. But the Giants' servants, symbols of materialism and tastelessness, do not want Ilse's poetic play. They demand entertainment, a song-and-dance routine, with no pretensions to high art. Although Cromo, the character actor, tries to persuade the others to acquiesce to the audience's demands, Ilse refuses. She attacks the audience for their ignorance and in their rage and intolerance she is torn to pieces behind the tattered curtain of her stage.

In his programme notes to the play, Strehler suggests that Pirandello schematized various modes of acting in the figures of Cotrone, Ilse and Cromo. Ilse, he argues, is "the mission carried out, the martyrdom." She represents an ideal of high art that sees itself as divorced from practical considerations, and is dedicated to the work in which she performs rather than to the needs of her audience. One is reminded of Eleonora Duse insisting on performing D'Annunzio's plays to dwindling audiences because she believed absolutely in their aesthetic value. Cromo, in contrast, represents "theatre-trade." He is a true professional, willing to supply whatever his audiences ask of him. Cotrone, who is not part of the company but one of the "Scalognati," is the actor-director for whom life is theatre. The "miracles" he creates are a means of coping with the wretchedness of existence. In act 2, he invites Ilse and her company to remain in the villa, and to try and look at the world with the eyes of belief in illusion:

> No need to reason any more! We live on that up here. We have nothing, but we have all the time in the world for ourselves; that's indescribable wealth, an absolute ferment of dreams. Things around us speak and have meaning only in the arbitrary way in

which we choose to alter them in our desperation. Our kind of desperation, mark you.

In the villa the inhabitants create their own illusions. Later in the same scene, Cotrone explains to Ilse that whilst the actors play their parts and make phantasms come to life, the "Scalognati" do the opposite and turn their own bodies into phantasms. As Strehler puts it: "Cotrone sums up all the possibilities of the theatre."

Strehler is suggesting that the play cannot be simply interpreted in terms of binary oppositions, a common pattern in much of Pirandello's earlier work. The issues are not presented through dichotomy, as, for example in *Six Characters,* nor is Pirandello so concerned with notions of relativity. *The Mountain Giants* is a play about the function of art, about the role it is able to play in a world of sadness and misery. Cotrone, on the one hand, and the group in the villa, represent what Strehler calls "pure theatre," the creative spirit that springs straight from the poet's mind. Ilse and the actors represent the theatre of actors: performance theatre. They take a text and interpret it, but they do not create that text prior to the performance. Strehler points out that this kind of distinction reflects the distinction between text and performance, the two components that together make up theatre.

Ilse and her company are taking a playtext around in search of an audience, but Cotrone has withdrawn from audiences, and thus withdrawn from any attempt to communicate with the world outside the villa. As he explains to the others in section 2, he has given up and removed himself from all the trappings of human society:

> Look at the earth, what a sad and sorry sight! Maybe there's someone down there who's under the delusion that he's living our life; but it isn't true, of course. Not one of us is in the body that another person sees us in; we're in the soul that speaks from God knows where. No-one can know that. Appearance after appearance with this ridiculous name of Cotrone . . . and him, with the name of Doccia . . . or Quaqueo. . . . A body is death: shadow and stone. Woe to anyone who thinks he can see himself in his body and his name!

Cotrone refers, throughout the play, to the innocence of animals and children, directly linking loss of innocence to growth of reason. Elsewhere in his writing, as in *The Rules of the Game,* for example, Pirandello had examined the sterility produced by a life based on reason. Cotrone has tried to escape from that sterility, into a world of his own making, a world in which heavenly beings can descend to earth, puppets can move and speak, dead men can return to life again. When Ilse begins to recite her part in section 3, she is joined by two characters, images that Cotrone tells her have materialized directly out of the imagination of the writer whose words she speaks. Again and again Cotrone warns against the deadening effects of reason and logical explanation. Existence can only be made tolerable, he suggests, by putting aside rationality and accepting what occurs without question.

In a different way, Ilse and the actors are also in revolt against rationality, but their revolt is one which causes pain and ultimately, death. When the actors first appear and tell Cotrone and the Scalognati about their play, Cromo describes the dead poet's work as a "cancer that has eaten us down to the bone." Ilse's sense of mission has become a fanaticism as extreme as that of Sirio Dossi in *Diana and Tuda*. It has become an obsession so total that eventually she dies for it, without ever understanding the meaning of Cotrone's remark about the dead poet: "Anyone who's a poet writes poems and doesn't kill himself." Ilse is, in a way, Tuda, continuing the struggle after the death of the artist. "I have given to his work the life that he was denied," she tells Cotrone. She sees herself as a life-bringer, the bearer of a special message that can transcend death; significantly the play she is trying to perform is a fairy story about a mother and child. In *The New Colony*, the mother figure was saved, but in this play not even she survives. There is no *deus ex machina* in *The Mountain Giants* to bring about a final climax, for this is probably Pirandello's most consciously dialectical play.

Strehler has pointed out the way in which this play discusses the relationship between text and performance, and between different attitudes to theatre. What the play also deals with is the vast complex area of communication in the theatre. Cromo, as the actor willing to play whatever he is asked, turns theatre into a commodity for the consumption of mass audiences. Ilse, in contrast, sees her own relationship with the text as pre-eminent and fails to understand the need to establish any basis for mass communication. Cotrone, as he admits, has opted out of the whole business of trying to communicate. In rejecting civilization as he knows it, he can afford to create a separate, introspective world for himself and the "Scalognati," beyond institutionalization.

In opting out of the struggle, refusing to put himself in the position that eventually kills Ilse, Cotrone emerges as a more likeable kind of Hinkfuss character, one whose antirationality arouses our sympathy. Ilse, in comparison, is the suffering, fanatical figure whose obsession with her ideal of pure art finally destroys her. But Ilse is in search of an ideal, she suffers for it and finally dies for it; the nobility of her actions, which are motivated by love, stands in contrast to Cotrone's retreat from the world. Ilse's nobility contrasts also with the baseness of her destroyers—the servants of the Giants, sent down the mountain because their masters were too busy with "important matters."

In *The Mountain Giants* there is no straightforward right and wrong position. Cotrone's case is presented sympathetically and we are invited to consider the validity of his views by reflecting on the squalid inadequacies of the world as we know it. Ilse, the female protagonist, is almost driven mad by her obsession, but she represents the case for the continuation of the institution of art. Both she and Cotrone make theatre, but only Ilse and her actors see theatre as necessarily involving a text, performers, a playing space and a public. That they disagree on the priority of those elements is another issue, for the fact remains that they try to continue a tradition and have not chosen an easy road into a world determined by their own exigencies and desires.

Through this play Pirandello seems to be debating with himself, between the needs of the soul for space and boundless imagination, as expressed by Cotrone, and the responsibility of the artist to the life that inspires his work. Because it is his last play, and because it was unfinished when he died, subsequent readings of the play have been framed within that notion of incompleteness. It is easy to draw parallels with *The Tempest,* and to recall the popular belief that Prospero's final speech is a farewell to the theatre, for Cotrone is in many ways a Prospero figure, conjuring spirits from the air. But Prospero was continually plotting to rejoin the world and to take up his role in society, whereas Cotrone has put the world behind him.

Pirandello described *The Mountain Giants* as both the triumph and the tragedy of poetry. In an earlier letter to Marta Abba he stressed his belief in the play and his hope that its greatness would be recognized:

> With it I shall go down, all the way down into the very entrails
> of despair. If the public doesn't weep this time, it means their
> hearts are turned to stone.

The full force of that tragedy emerges if we consider *The Mountain Giants* as the culmination of Pirandello's work, as his final pronouncement on the role and function of art. For this is a play that offers no answers to the problems it raises, and the lack of answers reflects the impossibility of reconciling an ideal of art with a repressive ideological system. Pirandello tried hard to keep his art separate from his politics, but although he may have managed to avoid making overt political statements, he could not avoid the inevitable consequences of the dominance of a Fascist discourse. The intellectual game of playing life off against form in theatre terms gradually took on deeper implications in his work, as can be seen by the way in which the idea of struggle begins to be replaced by the idea of resignation to adverse circumstances. The characters in Pirandello's earlier plays argue, question, suffer and try to fight back, but the characters in the Myths are more fatalistic, resigned to the greater force of circumstance. Moreover, in the Myths there is always an ideal world of Nature that the individual, once removed from the corruption of modern society, might be able to inhabit—La Spera's island, Sara's farm, Cotrone's villa—a place of withdrawal from struggle.

It would be too simplistic to say that Pirandello's later plays represent a decline in his powers as a writer as his own personal disillusionment increased. What can be seen in the later plays is the tension resulting from the incompatibility of an art form that originates from questioning and an ideology based on an ideal of authoritarian order. On the one hand Pirandello was trying to create a universal theatre, whilst on the other hand he was making public statements in support of Mussolini's invasion of Abyssinia. In his final plays the absurd size of the gulf between those two elements in his life can clearly be seen. The helplessness of Pirandello as man and artist is the silent text that we are now able to decipher in his work.

Chronology

1867	Luigi Pirandello born in Agrigento, Sicily, on June 28, to Stefano Pirandello, a prosperous businessman, and Caterina Ricci-Gramitti.
1886–1887	After completing his secondary education at the classical liceo, enrolls at the University of Palermo to study law; transfers to the Faculty of Letters at the University of Rome.
1888–1891	Studies philology at the University of Bonn and writes the poems later collected in *Elegie Renane* and *Pasqua di Gea*.
1892	In Rome, writes for various literary magazines.
1894	Marries Maria Antonietta Portulano, daughter of father's business partner. *Amori senza amore* (first collection of short stories). *Pier Gudrò*.
1896	Translation of Goethe's *Rome Elegies*.
1897	Part-time teacher of literature at a women's business college.
1898	*L'epilogo* (first play).
1901	*L'esclusa* (first novel).
1902	*Il turno* (novel).
1903	Pirandello's father and father-in-law lose everything when their sulfur mines are destroyed. Financial difficulties force Pirandello to take various teaching and tutoring jobs. Antonietta suffers the first of many psychological breakdowns.
1904	*Il fu Mattia Pascal* (novel).
1908	"Arte e scienza" and "L'umorismo" (literary essays).
1909	*I vecchi e i giovani* (novel).
1910	Two plays, *La morsa* (revision of *L'epilogo*) and *Lumìe di Sicilia*, performed in Rome; *Vita nuda* (stories) published.

1915   Mother dies. Son Stefano is sent to the front as Italy enters the war against Austria and Germany and is taken prisoner. Antonietta grows worse. Period of collaboration with Sicilian actor-directors Angelo Musco and Nino Martoglio begins.

1916   *Liolà, Il berretto a sonagli,* and *Pensaci, Giacomino!* first performed; *Si gira* (novel).

1917   *Così è (se vi pare), La giara,* and *Il piacere dell'onestà* first performed.

1918   *Il giuoco delle parti* and *Ma non è una cosa seria* first performed. Collected plays published as *Maschere nude.* Antonietta is placed in a psychiatric hospital.

1919   *L'innesto; L'uomo, la bestia, e la virtù;* and *La patente* first performed.

1920   *Tutto per bene; Come prima, meglio di prima;* and *La signora Morli, una e due* first performed.

1921   *Sei personaggi in cerca d'autore* first performed in Rome to an outraged audience.

1922   *Enrico IV* and *L'imbecille* first performed. *Six Characters* performed in London and New York. Adriano Tilgher, critic and friend of Pirandello, publishes the first and perhaps most influential study of Pirandello's theatre.

1923   Georges Pitoëff directs *Six Characters* in Paris; the production is extremely successful. *L'uomo dal fiore in bocca, La vita che ti diedi,* and *L'altro figlio* first performed.

1925   *Uno, nessuno, e centomila,* novel. *Six Characters* rewritten and published with an extensive preface. Pirandello founds the Teatro d'Arte in Rome. Beginning of collaboration and intimate friendship with actress Marta Abba.

1927   *Diana e la Tuda* first performed.

1928   *La nuova colonia* first performed. The Teatro d'Arte is dissolved.

1929   *O di uno o di nessuno* and *Lazzaro* first performed. Becomes member of the Accademia d'Italia.

1930   *Stasera si recita a soggetto* first performed.

1932   *Trovarsi* first performed.

1933   *Quando si è qualcuno* first performed.

1934   Nobel Prize for literature. *La favola del figlio cambiato* first performed.

1935   *Non si sa come* first performed. *I giganti della montagna* begun but completed only up to the second of three acts.

1936   Pirandello dies in Rome on December 10.

1937   Performance of *The Mountain Giants* produced by Marta Abba in Florence.

Contributors

HAROLD BLOOM, Sterling Professor of the Humanities at Yale University, is the author of *The Anxiety of Influence, Poetry and Repression,* and many other volumes of literary criticism. His forthcoming study, *Freud: Transference and Authority,* attempts a full-scale reading of all of Freud's major writings. A MacArthur Prize Fellow, he is general editor of five series of literary criticism published by Chelsea House. During 1987–88, he served as Charles Eliot Norton Professor of Poetry at Harvard University.

FRANCIS FERGUSSON taught at Bennington, Rutgers, and Princeton. He is the author of *The Human Image in Dramatic Literature, Shakespeare: The Pattern in his Carpet,* and *Dante's Dream of the Mind.*

ERIC BENTLEY is the Cornell Professor of Theatre at the State University of New York at Buffalo. The editor of numerous anthologies of drama and drama criticism, he is the author of *The Playwright as Thinker, In Search of Theatre,* and *Theatre of War,* as well as studies of Shaw and Brecht.

DANTE DELLA TERZA, Chairman of the Department of Romance Languages at Harvard University, is the author of *Ambiguità del comico.*

RICHARD GILMAN, Professor of Drama at the Yale Drama School, was the drama critic for *Commonweal* and the literary editor for *The New Republic.* He is the author of *The Confusion of Realms* and *Common and Uncommon Masks.*

ANNE PAOLUCCI, University Research Professor at Saint John's University (Canada), is the author of *From Tension to Tonic: The Plays of Edward Albee* and *Pirandello's Theatre: The Recovery of the Modern Stage for Dramatic Art,* as well as numerous articles on modern theatre.

GIOVANNI SINICROPI is Professor of Romance and Classical Languages at the University of Connecticut at Storrs. He has published a critical edition

165

of Giovanni Sercambi's *Novelle* and numerous articles on Ugo Foscolo, Boccaccio, Lope de Vega, and Giovanni Verga.

DOUGLAS RADCLIFF-UMSTEAD, Professor of Romance Languages at Kent State University, is the author of *Comedy in Renaissance Italy* and *Ugo Foscolo*.

OLGA RAGUSA is Chairman of the Italian Department at Columbia University and an editor of *Italica*.

MAURICE VALENCY is Professor of Dramatic Literature at Columbia University and Director of Academic Studies at The Juilliard School. A foremost critic of modern drama, he is the author of *The Flower and the Castle, The Breaking String,* and *The Cart and the Trumpet*.

SUSAN BASSNETT-McGUIRE is a lecturer in the Graduate School of Comparative Literature at the University of Warwick. She is the editor of *Comparison*.

Bibliography

Bassnett-McGuire, Susan. "Art and Life in Luigi Pirandello's *Questa sera si recita a soggetto*." In *Drama and Mimesis,* edited by James Redmond, 81–102. Vol. 2 of *Themes in Drama.* Cambridge: Cambridge University Press, 1980.

Bentley, Eric. *The Playwright as Thinker*, 145–55. New York: Harcourt, Brace, 1946.

———. *"Six Characters in Search of an Author"* (previously titled "Father's Day"). In *Theatre of War*, 45–63. New York: Viking, 1972.

Berlin, Normand. *A Secret Cause,* 109–25. Amherst: University of Massachusetts Press, 1981.

Bishop, Thomas. *Pirandello and the French Theatre.* New York: New York University Press, 1960.

Brose, Margaret. "Structures of Ambiguity in Pirandello's *Liolà.*" *Yale Italian Studies* 2 (1978): 115–42.

Brustein, Robert. "Luigi Pirandello." In *The Theatre of Revolt,* 279–318. Boston: Little, Brown, 1964.

Büdel, Oscar. *Pirandello.* New York: Hillary House, 1966.

Cambon, Glauco, ed. *Pirandello: A Collection of Critical Essays.* Englewood Cliffs, N.J.: Prentice-Hall, 1967.

Carrabino, Victor. "Claudel and Pirandello: Presence and Absence of God." *Claudel Studies* 7, no. 2 (1980): 18–28.

Charney, Maurice. "Shakespearean and Pirandellian: *Hamlet* and *Six Characters in Search of an Author.*" *Modern Drama* 24 (1981): 323–29.

Dombroski, Robert. "The Form of Chaos in Pirandello's *I vecchi e i giovani.*" *Yale Italian Studies* 2 (1978): 85–114.

Gaggi, Silvio. "Brecht, Pirandello and Two Traditions of Self-Critical Art." *Theatre Quarterly* 8, no. 2 (1979): 42–46.

Giudice, Gaspare. *Pirandello: A Biography.* Translated by Alastair Hamilton. London: Oxford University Press, 1975.

Gramsci, Antonio. "Il teatro di Pirandello." In *Letteratura e vita nazionale.* Turin: Einaudi, 1950.

Haller, Hermann. "Stylistic Trends in the Making of Pirandello's *Novelle per un anno.*" *Italica* 52 (1975): 273–90.

167

Hildebrand, Olle. "Pirandello's Theatre and the Influence of Nicolai Evreinov." *Italica*
    60 (1983): 107–39.
Illiano, Antonio. "Momenti e problemi di critica pirandelliana: *L'umorismo,* Pirandello
    e Croce, Pirandello e Tilgher." *PMLA* 83 (1968): 135–43.
Kernan, Alvin B. "Truth and Dramatic Mode in the Modern Theatre: Chekhov,
    Pirandello, and Williams." *Modern Drama* 1 (1958): 101–14.
Lepschy, Anna Laura. "Notes on the Figure of the Actor in Pirandello." *Yearbook
    of the British Pirandello Society* 1 (1981): 1–18.
Liebler, Naomi Conn. " 'Give o'er the play': Closure in Shakespeare's *Hamlet* and
    Pirandello's *Six Characters in Search of an Author.*" *Modern Drama* 24 (1981):
    314–22.
Lorch, Jennifer. "The 1925 Text of *Sei personaggi in cerca d'autore* and Pitoëff's
    Production of 1923." *Yearbook of the British Pirandello Society* 2 (1982): 32–46.
Matthaei, Renate. *Luigi Pirandello.* Translated by Simon and Erika Young. New York:
    Ungar, 1973.
Modern Drama 20, no. 4 (1977). Special Pirandello issue.
Newberry, Wilma. "Echegaray and Pirandello." *PMLA* 81 (1966): 123–29.
Paolucci, Anne. "Pirandello and the Waiting Stage of the Absurd (with Some
    Observations on a New 'Critical Language')."*Modern Drama* 23 (1980): 102–11.
————— *Pirandello's Theatre: The Recovery of the Modern Stage for Dramatic Art.*
    Carbondale: Southern Illinois University Press, 1974.
Procaccini, Alfonso. "Pirandello and the Enigma of Non-sense." *Quaderni
    d'Italianistica* 3 (1982): 51–62.
Ragusa, Olga. "Correlated Terms in Pirandello's Concept of Umorismo." In *The Two
    Hesperias: Literary Studies in Honor of Joseph G. Fucilla,* edited by Americo
    Bugliani, 291–307. Madrid: Porrua Taranzas, 1977.
—————. "Pirandello's 'Teatro d'Arte' and a New Look at his Fascism." *Italica* 55
    (1978): 236–53.
Rosenberg, Marvin. "Pirandello's Mirror." *Modern Drama* 6 (1964): 331–45.
Schlueter, June. *Metaphysical Characters in Modern Drama,* 19–34. New York:
    Columbia University Press, 1979.
Sciascia, Leonardo. *Pirandello e pirandellismo.* Caltanisetta: S. Sciascia, 1953.
Starkie, Walter. *Luigi Pirandello.* London: J. M. Dent, 1926. Berkeley: University
    of California Press, 1965.
Stewens, Dorothea. "The Character as Director: From 'Leonora Addio' to *Questa
    sera si recita a soggetto.*" *Yearbook of the British Pirandello Society* 2 (1982):
    66–72.
Styan, J. L. *The Dark Comedy,* 137–57. Cambridge: Cambridge University Press,
    1962.
—————. "Pirandellian Theatre Games: Spectator as Victim." *Modern Drama* 23
    (1980): 95–101.
—————. "Pirandello and the Teatro Grottesco." In *Symbolism, Surrealism and the
    Absurd,* 76–84. Vol. 2 of *Modern Drama in Theory and Practice.* Cambridge:
    Cambridge University Press, 1981.
Théâtre en Europe 10 (1986). Special Pirandello issue.
Tillona, Zina. "Pirandello's *Liolà:* A Variation on a Theme by Verga." *Italica* 52
    (1975): 262–71.

Vittorini, Domenico. *The Drama of Luigi Pirandello*. Philadelphia: University of
    Pennsylvania Press, 1935. New York: Russell & Russell, 1969.
Williams, Raymond. *Modern Tragedy*. London: Verso Editions, 1979.
World Theatre 16, no. 3 (1967). Special Pirandello issue.

Acknowledgments

"Action as Theatrical: *Six Characters in Search of an Author*" by Francis Fergusson from *The Idea of a Theater* by Francis Fergusson, © 1949, 1977 by Princeton University Press. Reprinted by permission of Princeton University Press.

"*Enrico IV*: The Tragic Emperor" (originally entitled "*Enrico IV*") by Eric Bentley from *Tulane Drama Review* 10, no. 3 (Spring 1966), © 1966 by *Tulane Drama Review*. Reprinted by permission by the MIT Press Journals.

"On Pirandello's Humorism" by Dante della Terza from *Veins of Humor*, edited by Harry Levin, © 1972 by the President and Fellows of Harvard College. Reprinted by permission.

"Pirandello" by Richard Gilman from *The Making of Modern Drama* by Richard Gilman, © 1972, 1973, 1974 by Richard Gilman. Reprinted by permission of Farrar, Straus & Giroux, Inc.

"Comedy and Paradox in Pirandello's Plays (An Hegelian Perspective)" by Anne Paolucci from *Modern Drama* 20, no. 4 (December 1977), © 1977 by the University of Toronto, Graduate Centre for Study of Drama. Reprinted by permission of *Modern Drama*.

"The Metaphysical Dimension and Pirandello's Theatre" by Giovanni Sinicropi from *Modern Drama* 20, no. 4 (December 1977), © 1977 by the University of Toronto, Graduate Centre for Study of Drama. Reprinted by permission of *Modern Drama*.

"The Fugitive from Life" by Douglas Radcliff-Umstead from *The Mirror of Our Anguish* by Douglas Radcliff-Umstead, © 1978 by Associated University Presses, Inc. Reprinted by permission of Associated University Presses, Inc.

"Early Drama" (originally entitled "Early Narrative and Drama") by Olga Ragusa from *Luigi Pirandello* by Olga Ragusa, © 1980 by Olga Ragusa. Reprinted by permission of Edinburgh University Press.

"Pirandello: A New Conception of Theatre" (originally entitled "Pirandello") by

Index

173